Space Saving Shelves and Built-ins

Jay Hedden

Ideals Publishing Corp.
Milwaukee, Wisconsin

Table of Contents

ISBN 0-8249-6104-8 395

Copyright © 1981 by Ideals Publishing Corporation

Published by Ideals Publishing Corporation
11315 Watertown Plank Road
Milwaukee, Wisconsin 53226

Editor, David Schansberg

Cover photo courtesy of Georgia Pacific.

◻ SUCCESSFUL
HOME IMPROVEMENT SERIES

Bathroom Planning and Remodeling
Kitchen Planning and Remodeling
Space Saving Shelves and Built-ins
Finishing Off Additional Rooms
Finding and Fixing the Older Home
Money Saving Home Repair Guide
Homeowner's Guide to Tools
Homeowner's Guide to Electrical Wiring
Homeowner's Guide to Plumbing
Homeowner's Guide to Roofing and Siding
Homeowner's Guide to Fireplaces
Home Plans for the '80s
How to Build Your Own Home

Kitchen Cabinets

When you think of cabinets in a home, it's the kitchen that comes to mind first. This room generally requires the most cabinets, as well as cabinets with the greatest variety of functions.

Some kitchen cabinets contain a cooking range (cooktop), others the oven. Modern microwave ovens may be in a separate cabinet, or may share the same cabinet as the regular oven. Depending on personal preference the microwave may be above or below the regular oven.

The sink is in a cabinet of its own and may have a single, double or even triple basin. Some double-basin units will have one deep and one shallow basin; others will have basins of equal depth. If a sink includes a garbage-disposal unit, there must be space for it under the cabinet.

Dishwashers are fitted under a countertop in a base cabinet, usually next to or very close to the sink. This allows for the shortest run of water pipes and drains.

Planning

Because so much work is carried out in a kitchen, planning its layout is the first and most important step when building kitchen cabinets. However, our aim is to tell you how to build those cabinets once you have determined the plan. For how to plan a kitchen layout, we suggest *Kitchen Planning and Remodeling*.

When remodeling a kitchen, the sink counter should be completed first to enable its prompt use. This means that the line of base cabinets in which the sink is located will have to be completed, and the top installed, in a minimum of time.

The second section to be worked on should be the cooktop, which may be in the same cabinet as the sink. You will probably not have to go without access to your cooking area for very long.

Before you begin installing the cabinets for the sink, cooktop, range or oven, have the proper specifications for these appliances. The instructions from the manufacturer show how the appliance is to be installed, and where the partitions and shelves must be located to allow the appliance to fit properly. An oven, for example, must be wired and fitted so it can be pulled out of its cabinet when work on it is necessary.

Some cooktop ranges are shallow, others are deep and may include a downdraft exhaust fan. Space must be allowed in the base cabinet below, as specified for the appliance.

As with any cabinet, kitchen cabinets are basically simple boxes; just make sure the boxes are the right size and shape.

Plywood generally is used, and where it will show, the hardwood-veneered type is preferred. Interior partitions and shelves can be ordinary fir plywood, which helps keep down the cost.

Most kitchen cabinets are made of birch plywood. This is a light-colored wood, and fairly grain-free. It takes stain readily and can be finished to simulate other kinds of wood. Birch plywood, as is the case with most hardwood-plywoods, has a "good" side and a "bad" or "off" side. That is, the one side is clear and straight-grained, while the other side may have some wild grain and perhaps stain streaks. We have found that using the "off" side can create some wonderful effects, because the strong grain gives an unusual character to the surfaces.

This character can be accented by using an unusual staining procedure: a bright green, blue, red or orange decorator stain is applied first. This type of stain actually is an analine dye, rather than an oil or water-based material. When the bright color has dried thoroughly, usually after 24 hours, a walnut penetrating sealer is applied.

The resulting finish is a dark walnut, with green, blue, red, or orange glowing through. The penetrating sealer not only provides the walnut color but is a finish itself, so varnish or lacquer is not required as a final coat.

Construction—Base Cabinets

Base cabinets for a kitchen can be built in one of two ways. The first method is to build the cabinet using all ¾-inch plywood, with the cabinet ends and partitions the same height so all contact the floor. Shelves are fitted in dadoes cut in the inner faces of the ends, and on both sides of the partitions. Dadoes in the ends are ⅜ inch deep, which is half the thickness of the ¾-inch plywood. When shelves are in line on the partitions, the dadoes are ³⁄₁₆ inch deep on each side, leaving ⅜ inch of plywood for support. When they are not in line, the dadoes should be the standard ⅜ inch deep.

The bottom shelf of the base cabinet, which actually is the bottom of the cabinet, is positioned 1 inch above the top of the toe-space notch. A full-length facing, cut from 1 x 2 stock, forms the bottom of the cabinet spacing and hides the space between the cabinet bottom and the lower ends of the partitions and the end uprights. Note that this piece of facing is part of the facing frame that is attached as a complete assembly.

There arises a potential problem at this point: the lower facing should be positioned so its upper edge is flush with the top of the bottom cabinet shelf. The ¾-inch thickness of the shelf and the 1-inch space between the shelf and toe space can add up to 1¾ inches. This is the width of the "old-fashioned" 1 x 2 (¾ x 1¾ inches). If you use some of the newer stock, a 1 x 2 will measure just ¾ x 1½ inches. Check the width of the 1 x 2 stock you buy, and if it is only 1½ inches wide, make the dadoes for the bottom shelf only ¾ inch (rather than 1 inch) above the toe-space notch.

A length of 1 x 4 stock (which measures ¾ x 3½ inches) is nailed to the front edges of the ends and partitions of the base cabinet at the back of the toe space. This 1 x 4 is the "stretcher" that ties the ends and partitions together. It is easiest to face-nail the stretcher to the front edges of the partitions, but you might want the ends of the stretcher not to show at the end of the cabinet. In this case, make the toe-

space notch in the cabinet ends ¾ inch shorter, back to front, than the notch in the partitions. Since the stretcher is cut shorter by the width of the ends, it will fit inside the ends. You then can nail through the ends of the base cabinet into the ends of the stretcher. Where one end of a base cabinet is against a wall, this modification could be made only on the open end. This might seem obvious, but we'll say it now and repeat it every once in a while: measure twice and cut once. You can always shorten a piece of wood, but there is no practical way to lengthen it.

This same kind of inside fitting can be used at the lower back of a base cabinet for the 1 x 4 or 2 x 4 used there, and also for the 1 x 4 strip used at the upper back of a base cabinet.

Before joining the plywood ends and partitions, make dadoes for the required shelves. Or glue and nail 1 x 2 cleats to the inside of the ends and on both sides of partitions. If you want to spend a little more time and money, use shelf brackets that permit adjustment of the shelf levels.

The second basic construction method for kitchen base cabinets is to make a frame of 2 x 4s that sets on the floor and cover it with hardwood-faced plywood. The cabinet ends are nailed to it, as is the cabinet bottom. Partitions are cut to fit on top of the cabinet bottom. The front 2 x 4 for the floor frame is set back ¾ inch, so that a facing of 1 x 4 stock can be nailed to it. Stock 2 x 4s are not finished lumber, and are primarily used as construction members. You can buy top-grade 1 x 4 stock for the facing used as the back of the toe space, or use a strip of hardwood-

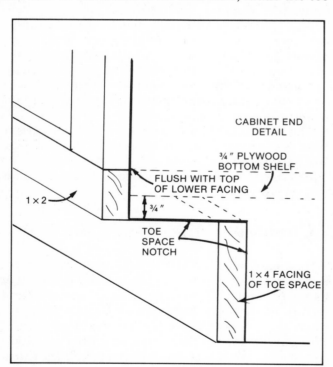

The most common way to build kitchen cabinets (and cabinets for other rooms) is to make them completely of ¾-inch plywood, with ends and partitions that sit on the floor. Dadoes are cut in the ends and in the partitions to accept shelves. Wooden cleats can be used to support shelves, or special shelf hardware can be installed to permit space adjustment between shelves.

These birch cabinets have been finished with a dark walnut stain to the strong grain.

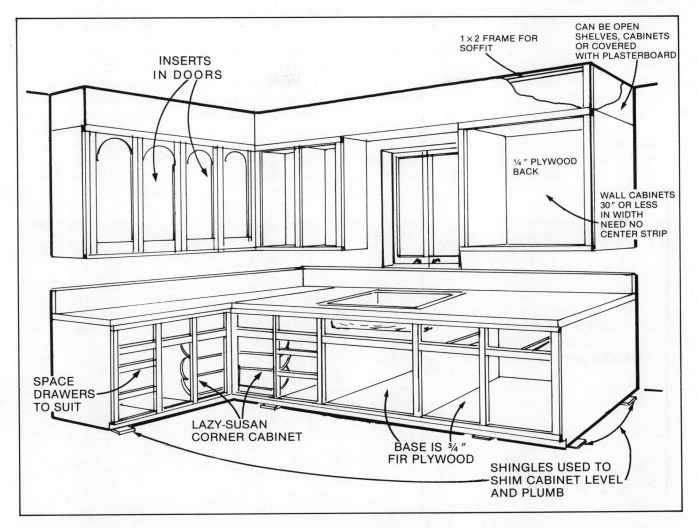

INSERTS
IN DOORS

1 × 2 FRAME FOR
SOFFIT

CAN BE OPEN
SHELVES, CABINETS
OR COVERED
WITH PLASTERBOARD

¼ " PLYWOOD
BACK

WALL CABINETS
30" OR LESS
IN WIDTH
NEED NO
CENTER STRIP

SPACE
DRAWERS
TO SUIT

LAZY-SUSAN
CORNER CABINET

BASE IS ¾ "
FIR PLYWOOD

SHINGLES USED TO
SHIM CABINET LEVEL
AND PLUMB

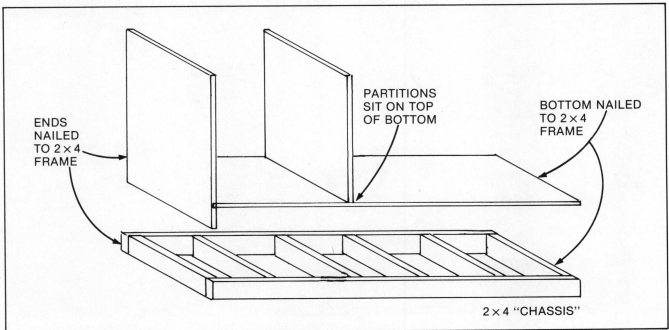

PARTITIONS
SIT ON TOP
OF BOTTOM

BOTTOM NAILED
TO 2 × 4
FRAME

ENDS
NAILED
TO 2 × 4
FRAME

2 × 4 "CHASSIS"

The second method of building cabinets is with a 2 x 4 "chassis" which provides a rigid platform that allows cabinets to be moved from one location to another with minimum chance of racking or twisting.

faced plywood, as used for the rest of the base cabinet.

The front-to-back members of the 2 x 4 frame are located at the ends, under each partition and about every 24 inches in between.

Shelf arrangements are the same as for the first type of cabinet construction.

The first type of cabinet generally has enough strength and rigidity to fit most situations, but the second type of construction is chosen when cabinets are built at one location and moved to another for installation. The 2 x 4 "chassis" assures that the cabinet assembly will not easily be racked or distorted out of shape. This also holds true when the cabinet is shimmed to be plumb and level when it is installed.

Shims used to level and plumb cabinets are ordinary second-course shingles. This kind of shingle is less expensive than first-course shingles. They may have knots and other imperfections, which make no difference as they are not seen.

Note that the cabinets are shimmed level and plumb before the facing strip at the back of the toe space is applied. The strip hides the shingles.

You can add shelves in areas you never even thought of: above the kitchen sink to provide growing space for your herb garden, or above windows to store decorative cook-ware that is difficult to store in a cabinet. Photo courtesy of Armstrong Cork

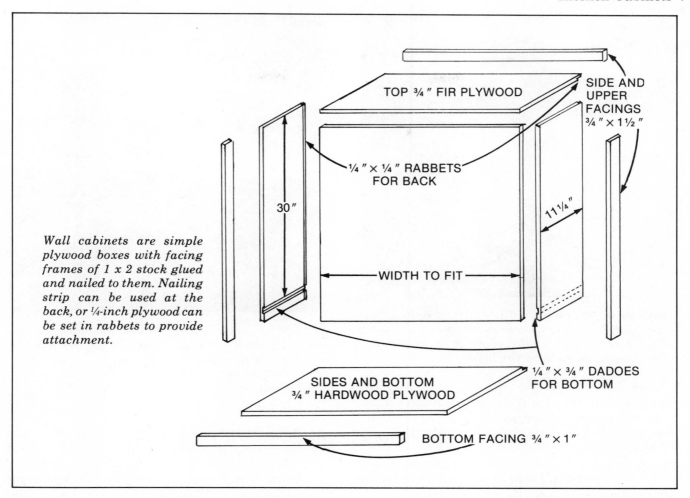

TOP ¾" FIR PLYWOOD

SIDE AND UPPER FACINGS ¾" × 1½"

¼" × ¼" RABBETS FOR BACK

30"

11¼"

Wall cabinets are simple plywood boxes with facing frames of 1 x 2 stock glued and nailed to them. Nailing strip can be used at the back, or ¼-inch plywood can be set in rabbets to provide attachment.

WIDTH TO FIT

SIDES AND BOTTOM ¾" HARDWOOD PLYWOOD

¼" × ¾" DADOES FOR BOTTOM

BOTTOM FACING ¾" × 1"

Construction—Wall Cabinets

Wall cabinets for a kitchen are simple plywood boxes, on the fronts of which are glued and nailed facing frames assembled from 1 x 2 stock. The assembly is much the same as base cabinets, including a back stretcher that usually is a 1 x 4. This stretcher provides a means of nailing or screwing the wall cabinets to the wall studs.

In most cases, no backs are installed in kitchen cabinets. The wall of the house is the back of the cabinets. You might prefer to have a back of ¼-inch plywood or hardboard to prevent the relatively soft plasterboard or plaster from being damaged from items stored in the cabinets. This will require a ¼ x ¼-inch rabbet on the inner back edges of the ends of the cabinets, and partitions will have to be shortened ¼ inch at the back to allow for the thickness of the plywood. Ready-made cabinets have backs to help strengthen the assembly.

Cabinets can be purchased in kit form. You get a box of pieces and parts that you take home and assemble with glue and screws or nails. The very practical reason for retailers selling these kits is that they have found that preassembled unfinished

furniture of all kinds, including cabinets, are often damaged in shipping. Further damage can occur when the items are on display in the store. A flat package of material seldom is damaged, requires little storage space and is easy to carry home in the back seat of a car.

A money-saving way of installing a roomful of cabinets is to combine ready-made units and cabinets you make yourself. You can buy the doors and drawer fronts of ready-made units and fit them to cabinets you have built yourself.

Cabinet Doors

The overall styling of cabinets is largely determined by the doors and drawer fronts, plus decorative hardware and surface ornamentation. These various factors must be coordinated, as you certainly would not use rustic Early-American hinges with a French Provincial style of door or drawer front.

There are four basic types of doors. All can be used on both wall and base cabinets.

• The lip type overlaps the frame all around. A rabbet is cut on the back edges of the door so the door

Cabinets in this pantry off the kitchen have overlay doors that cover framing and touch almost edge-to-edge. Where drawers are installed above doors, fronts again almost touch, as do the doors below.

A flush-type door is hung in an opening, with just enough clearance to swing freely. Hinges are recessed into edges of door and frame; even "invisible" hinges can be used so that none show. Photo courtesy of Azrock Floor Products

is recessed half its thickness into the facer frame. The front edges of the door usually are rounded, but can be left square or even given a profile with a shaper or router.

- The overlay type completely covers the face of the cabinet, whether wall or base cabinet. Overlay doors are made larger than the opening, and the edges of adjacent doors and drawers meet. This type of door is quite heavy and places a strain on the hinges and framing.
- The flush-type door is hung in the opening with minimum clearance. There is just enough clearance for the door to swing freely to open and close. Hinges are recessed into the edges of the door and the frame. Because the doors must be fitted in the

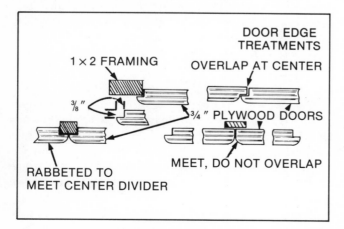

A lip-type door is the one most commonly used for base and wall cabinets. Various methods of fitting doors that meet in the opening are shown.

openings, they take more time to hang than other types. One variation of the flush type is to cover the complete front of the cabinet with a sheet of plywood, then to cut the doors and drawer fronts out of the sheet with a jig saw or portable circular saw. The doors then are hinged in the openings and the grain matches exactly. Any minor irregularities in the cuts are not easily seen because the edges of the cuts match perfectly. Because of the extra work, however, and the chance of spoiling a full sheet of plywood, this type of door is not often seen.

- Sliding doors are fine for some locations, such as above regular wall cabinets in what usually is a closed-in soffit, but only one-half the cabinet is accessible when a door is opened. Rabbeting the top and bottom of the doors permits them to fit together quite closely, minimizing entry of dust. When using power tools, make grooves in the top and bottom of the cabinet for the doors. The top groove should be twice the depth of the bottom groove so the doors can be slipped into the top groove and then swung in and the bottom dropped into the lower groove. If you have only hand tools, make the tracks by nailing 2 strips of quarter-round molding to the top and to the bottom of the cabinet. A ¼-inch strip between the pieces of quarter-round keeps the doors from rubbing together. The doors should project into the upper "track" only about ⅛ inch. Larger sliding doors are hung from metal brackets that run on an overhead

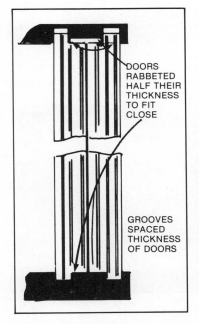

Rabbeting top and bottom of each door creates close-fitting sliding doors. The back edges of the front door are rabbeted, as are the front edges of the back door. This allows the doors to almost touch, so there is only a small gap that dust can enter. Be sure to seal edges, backs, and fronts of doors.

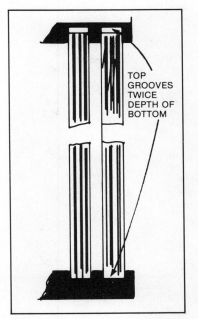

To make sliding doors removable, make bottom grooves 3/16 inch deep, the top ones 3/8 inch deep. Doors are inserted by pushing up into top groove, then dropping into bottom groove. If you make the top grooves for sliding doors twice the depth of bottom grooves, doors can be replaced and removed easily.

track, utilizing ball-bearing wheels. Both single and double-track sets of this hardware are available. The single track is used where the door would open by sliding along the adjacent wall, rather than bypassing another door which is the case with double-track hardware. The door bottoms are kept plumb and aligned with a T-shaped guide set in a hole in the floor. The guide fits in a groove cut in the bottom edge of the door.

The surface appearances of cabinet doors and drawer fronts can be varied in a number of ways, and the look can be slab, raised or recessed panel, ornamental molding and many other styles. Doors and drawers can even have cloth, glass, ceramic tile, metal or plastic inserts. Woven cane, usually used for chair seats and backs, is another material that can be employed to make an attractive and different surface.

Inserts in the doors and drawer fronts of some "decorator" kitchens are covered with wallpaper that matches or is compatible with the paper on the walls. The inserts are made of thin hardboard or plywood and can be removed so the covering can be replaced when the kitchen is redecorated.

Shutters also can be used for cabinet doors. You can buy these ready-made in many sizes, and there is no reason why you cannot make them part of your cabinet. Fixed-louver shutters are the least expensive and add a touch of style to your cabinets. Shutters with pivoting louvers are more costly, but are a good idea where ventilation is required for a cabinet.

Doors that run on tracks at the top are kept aligned at the bottom by T-shaped devices fitted in holes in the floor. The T-shape fits in a groove cut in the bottom of the door. If you have only hand tools, nail two lengths of quarter-round molding to the floor to provide a guide track. No center strip is required.

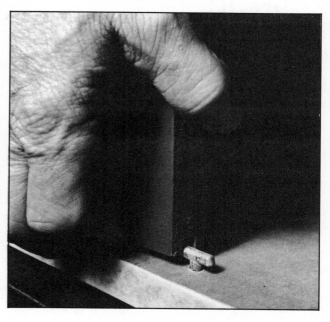

For easy moving, by-passing sliding doors, you can use hardware that consists of two metal brackets fastened to the top of each door. Nylon wheels with ball bearings roll in a two-lipped track fastened to the door frame with screws. For a single door there is a one-lip track. This setup is generally used for large cabinets and closets.

If you have only hand tools, you can make sliding doors by spacing ¼-inch quarter-round molding on either side of a strip that is ¼ inch square.

Construction

The most common cabinet door and drawer front is the simple lip-type slab with rounded edges and a rabbet on the back edges. The doors are made from ¾-inch plywood, generally with a hardwood veneer on the face, or from glued-up solid stock that has a net thickness of ¾ inch. The lip on the door overlaps ⅜ inch all around, which means the door must be ¾ inch longer than the cabinet opening, and ¾ inch wider. The same situation occurs for two doors that overlap across an opening that requires two doors. On one door the rabbet is reversed to match the rabbet on the other door where they overlap. A better arrangement is to have the doors meet on a stop strip, but not overlap.

The meeting edges need not be rabbeted and can simply contact a stop strip, or they can be rabbeted with a stop strip ⅜ inch closer to the front edge of the cabinet to keep the doors flush. Keep in mind that each door is only ⅜ inch wider than half the opening, to provide the ⅜-inch lip at the sides. The doors are a total of ¾ inch higher than the height of the opening, to provide for the upper and lower ⅜-inch lip.

Door edges can be shaped with a molding cutter on a table saw, a spindle shaper, or with a portable router. After the edges are shaped, you can create interest by sawing or routing shallow grooves parallel to the edges or by applying thin moldings.

Door inserts are covered with wallpaper to match that on the wall. Panels in these doors are the "raised" type, which means wallpaper would have to be stripped off when it comes time to redecorate the kitchen. Some doors have removable panels of hardboard or plywood. Photo courtesy of Thomas Strahan, Wallcovering Div. National Gypsum Co.

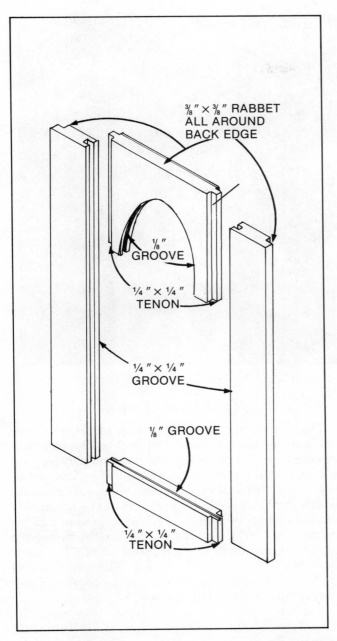

The basic framing for a cabinet door, with some kind of insert, is shown. Top, bottom, and side members of the frame can be varied to suit installation of various kinds of wood, metal, hardboard, and plastic panels.

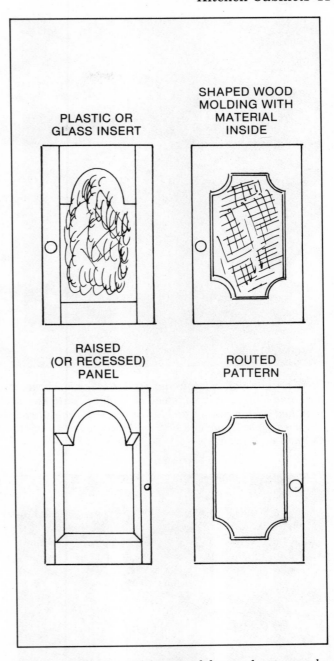

PLASTIC OR GLASS INSERT

SHAPED WOOD MOLDING WITH MATERIAL INSIDE

RAISED (OR RECESSED) PANEL

ROUTED PATTERN

Surface appearances of doors and drawer fronts may be varied in unlimited ways. Shown here are a few ways doors can be framed and inserts installed.

Hardware

It's easy to install the special hinges made for lip-type doors. They are called ⅜-inch offset hinges and are available in a wide variety of styles and finishes.

Latches come in several types, at several prices. Friction catches use rubber or plastic against metal to assure positive latching, and some types even are metal to metal; these are not too reliable, although inexpensive. Magnetic latches have the highest price, but are the most reliable. Be sure the magnetic latches you buy are the heavy-duty type. Light-duty magnetic latches have only about half the holding power of heavy-duty types and should be used only on very small doors.

It is a waste of time and money to build a beautiful cabinet, then to install cheap hardware. Latches or catches must operate every day, many times in some instances, and if the catch fails, that is what will be noticed, not the beauty or craftsmanship of the cabinet.

For a unique look in a colonial-style kitchen, door inserts are made of tin-plated steel or copper; patterns are punched with a nail or awl. These panels simulate panels used in antique pie safes. Photo courtesy of Tile Council of America

Translucent plastic panels are safer and minimize stress on doors and hinges more than traditional bottle glass inserts.

Cabinet Tops

The standard width of the tops of kitchen base cabinets is approximately 24 inches. We say "approximately" because the tops are made by ripping a 4 x 8-foot sheet of plywood lengthwise. The resulting two strips will be 24 inches each, less half the width of the saw blade. The kerf of the usual saw blade is about ⅛ inch, so each strip is about 23¹⁵⁄₁₆ inches wide. When a 1 x 2 is added to the front edge of the countertop to make it project by 1½ inches, it becomes ¾ inch or more thicker. The additional ¾ inch (or more) makes the width of the counter about 24¾ inches wide, front to back.

If a backsplash of ¾-inch plywood is used, the actual countertop approximates the original 24 inches. There may be instances when a counter depth of more than 24 inches would be useful, say when a small microwave oven was set on it. There is no reason why you can't make the counter as wide as you wish, but there are practical limitations. A counter more than 24 inches deep will require cabinets too deep for storing items that must be reached.

A practical solution to the problem is to have slide-out shelves or slide-out bins. Any shelf that is made to slide out should have a rim around the edge or a back piece to keep things from falling off the back; in effect, it would be a shallow bin.

Another problem with making a countertop wider than 24 inches is that you are left with a long, narrow piece of plywood. This piece can, however, be ripped to 18 inches and used for the sides and shelves in wall cabinets.

This cabinet countertop features ceramic tile that extends to the base of the wall cabinets providing an efficient, easy-to-clean work area. The board beneath the wall cabinets gives extra storage space for utensils, pots, and pans. Photo courtesy of American Olean Tile

Instead of adding 1 x 2s to the front edge of a cabinet top to make it project beyond the cabinets beneath, you may make the base cabinet ¾-inch (or more) narrower than the top. That is, cut the sides and partitions so the base cabinet is just 23¼ inches. Where space is a problem, this is the best answer. Very few people can use the full depth of kitchen cabinets efficiently, so a matter of ¾ inch makes little difference.

Standard height for kitchen base cabinets is 36 inches. This means that the ends and partitions should be 35¼ inches high, so when the ¾-inch plywood top is added, the total height will be 36 inches.

If the members of your family are shorter or taller than the average person, you might want to adjust height accordingly. Keep in mind that if you sell the house at some point, having cabinets 39 to 40 inches high for tall people, or 32 inches for short people, may restrict the sale of the house.

The solution to the problem is a compromise: build some cabinets high—or low—special counters for food-preparation centers or whatever the counter will be used for most. A low counter makes a handy baking center, as it is easier to knead bread dough or roll out piecrusts than on a standard height. A high counter suggests the use of a handy stool to ease kitchen work, such as peeling and cutting, or other chores that take a lot of time. Pull-out slabs make handy low counters and are great for blenders and mixers where the cook is working above the appliance. Locate such pull-outs about 30 inches above the floor; this is table height.

Tops for kitchen base cabinets should be purchased in one piece and installed after the cabinet is

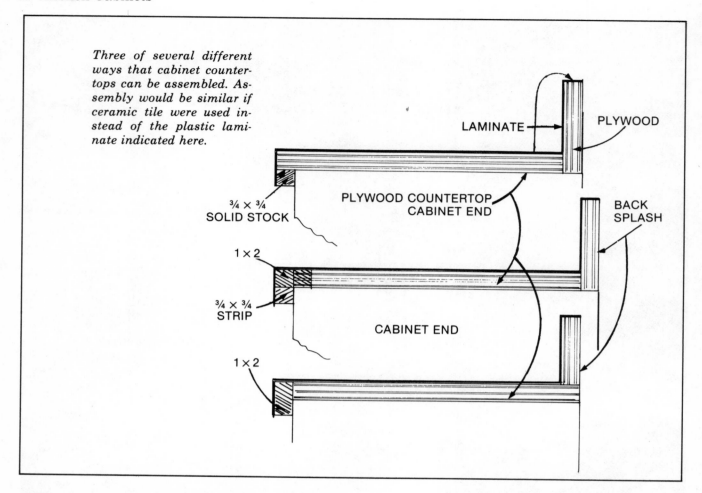

Three of several different ways that cabinet countertops can be assembled. Assembly would be similar if ceramic tile were used instead of the plastic laminate indicated here.

LAMINATE → PLYWOOD

PLYWOOD COUNTERTOP
CABINET END

BACK SPLASH

¾ × ¾ SOLID STOCK

1 × 2

¾ × ¾ STRIP

CABINET END

1 × 2

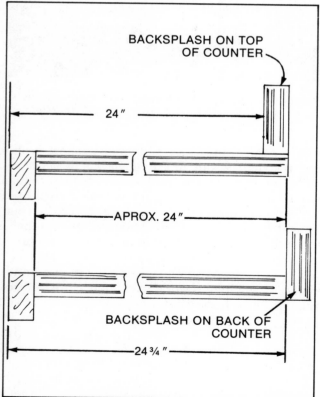

BACKSPLASH ON TOP OF COUNTER

24″

APROX. 24″

BACKSPLASH ON BACK OF COUNTER

24¾″

in place. Necessary joints can be made tight with devices made especially for this kind of assembly.

It is general practice, where possible, to cut the sink, built-in cooktop, and other openings after the countertop is installed. In this case the plastic laminate is applied after the countertop is in place.

If one of the cuts is too close to the backsplash to permit using the portable electric jig saw, then the top is first temporarily positioned and marked. It is then removed, the openings cut, and finally is replaced and fastened permanently in place. In this situation the top would have to be fastened by driving screws from underneath, up through the framing into the top. Some tops are attached by driving screws down through the plywood top into the framing; then the laminate is applied over the top to cover the screws.

If a backsplash is to be installed behind the countertop, plastic laminate is applied to the splash before it is installed to assure that the laminate will extend down behind the back edge of the countertop for a good seal. A metal or plastic strip can be fitted between the countertop and the backsplash to assure a tight joint, although if the job is done properly, and the back edge of the countertop has been cut straight, the strips are not necessary.

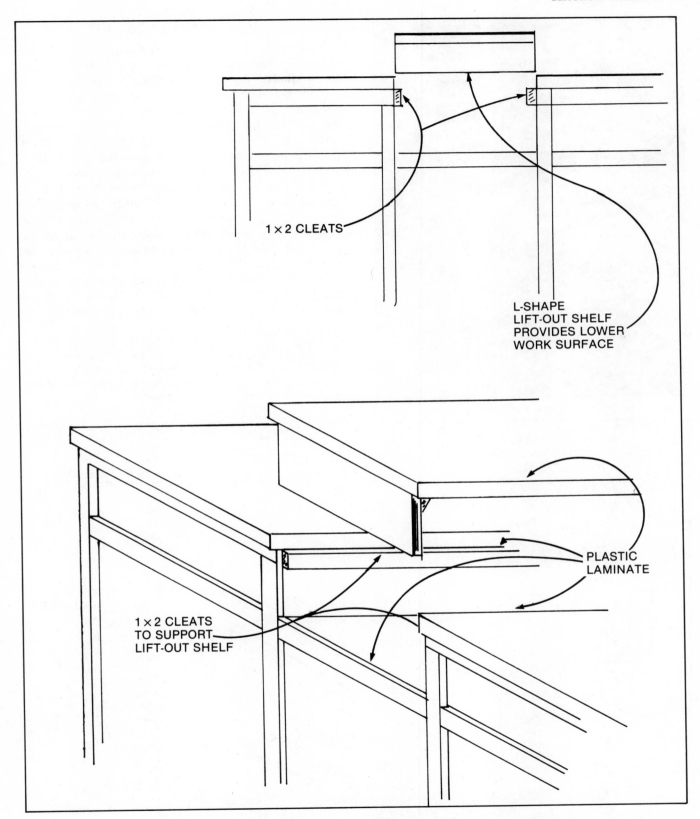

1 × 2 CLEATS

L-SHAPE
LIFT-OUT SHELF
PROVIDES LOWER
WORK SURFACE

PLASTIC
LAMINATE

1 × 2 CLEATS
TO SUPPORT
LIFT-OUT SHELF

One way to create a lower work surface for a shorter person is with a lift-off section of countertop. Lifting the section reveals a work surface covered with plastic laminate.

The L-shaped section is reinforced with a triangular glue block between the front, which can be a false drawer front, and the top. The ends of the countertop exposed when the section is removed are covered with plastic laminate, as are the sides of the "well," to assure easy cleaning. The top is supported on 1 x 2 cleats fitted on each side of the well as indicated.

Laminate

When plastic laminate is applied to a countertop, it is cemented to the front edge first, then trimmed to be flush with the upper surface of the top. This is called "self-edging." The laminate then is applied to the upper surface of the top, so it overlaps the upper edge of the laminate on the front. This creates a joint that is horizontal, rather than vertical, so there is less chance of liquid entering the joint.

Contact adhesive is used to apply plastic laminate. If you have never applied laminate, it is suggested you apply it to some small projects first, before trying the cabinet. Basically, the contact adhesive is brushed on the wood countertop and on the back side of the laminate and allowed to set. Depending on the brand, the adhesive may take 30 minutes or less to set. Read the instructions that come with the brand you buy, as they will tell you the "working time" of the adhesive. Some types will

If personal needs require counters that are lower or higher than the standard 36 inches, a slide-out or roll-out counter is one answer. This surface can slide in and out, or pivot, as shown in the drawing.

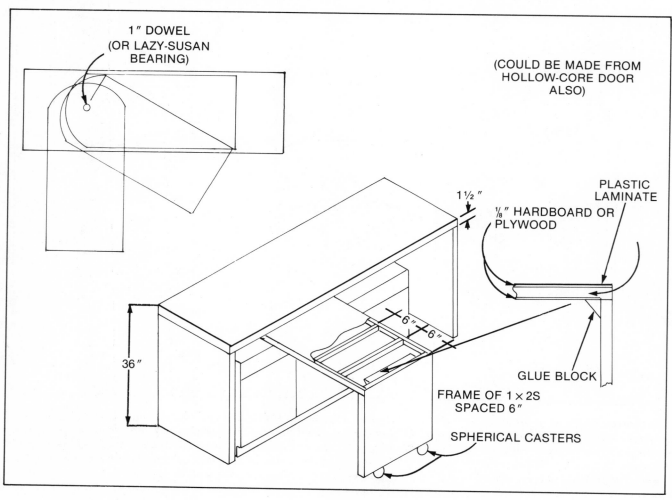

be adhesive one, two, or three hours after they have been applied. Others will require application of a second coat if the laminate is not applied within the specified time.

Brown wrapping paper and newspapers have been suggested for keeping the laminate and countertop separate until you have the laminate correctly positioned; however, you may find that paper can stick to one or more spots in the adhesive. A better way is to use ⅛-inch dowels or small metal rods, such as gas-welding rods. When the laminate is properly aligned, you pull out the rods one at a time.

The front edge of the plastic laminate applied to the top is cut about ⅛ inch to ¼ inch too long, so it can be trimmed flush with the front edge after the laminate is firmly attached. There are devices that can be used with a portable router for trimming laminate, but inexpensive hand tools can also be used effectively. There is no need to buy an expensive power tool if you are going to do only one counter job.

Contact adhesive grips immediately, as has often been stated, but not instantly. That is, if you are just a bit out of line, gently push the laminate in the direction you want to move it. Contact adhesive has a rubber base and it will give a bit. In an extreme case, where you have really slipped out of line, gently raise the laminate and cut away the stringy connections made by the adhesive between the lam-

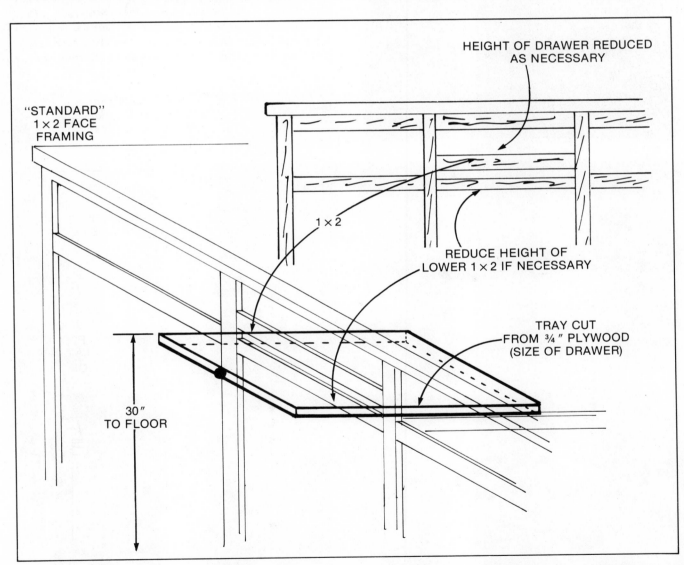

A slide-out shelf can be installed to provide a lower working surface. This requires that one drawer be made shallower than the rest—which makes it handy for silverware. A 1 x 2 piece of framing is positioned horizontally across the opening so there is a slot a fraction higher than ¾ inch that has been created. The shelf is a piece of ¾-inch plywood or an edge-glued assembly of solid stock, made to fit the opening. Screw a small cleat to the underside of the shelf after it has been slipped into the slot, to act as a stop so the shelf cannot be pulled out all the way.

inate and the countertop. If you have cut away too much of the adhesive, you would do better to peel the laminate free of the countertop and apply another layer of adhesive to both surfaces and then redo the job.

If you will use a ceramic tile on the countertop, apply with mastic, and seal the joints with grout. Openings are always cut prior to installation of the countertop. With ceramic tile, the hardest area to cut and fit is the back row of tiles. The front edge of the countertop is trimmed with L-shaped pieces of tile especially made for the application.

You can trim plastic laminate with special cutters in a portable electric router; however, inexpensive hand tools such as this Arlyn cutter, sold mail-order by Albert Constantine and Company (among others) does a neat job. It can be adjusted as necessary and has replaceable cutters.

Laminate covers cabinets, countertops, and the built-in dining area of this kitchen. The result is a kitchen that is attractive and very easy to clean. Photo courtesy of Azrock Floor Products

Drawers

Drawers for kitchen cabinets are assembled in a number of different ways, but the "standard" method is the best. The front and sides of the drawer are grooved to accept the bottom that generally is ⅛- or ¼-inch hardboard or plywood, and the back of the drawer sets on top of this bottom. The bottom is held only by a few brads or small nails driven up through it into the back. This allows the bottom to "float" as it expands and contracts with humidity instead of forcing the drawer apart. Make sure there is a bit of clearance all around the bottom—it should be a loose fit in the dadoes—so it can expand and contract.

A number of devices are available to make drawers slide more easily. Several factors should be considered before selecting a device: cost, intended use, and weight. A drawer that will be loaded with heavy pots and pans, for example, needs a smooth-working slide of some type. A lightweight drawer such as used in a kitchen desk could be installed with no slides at all. A simple centering guide would do the job.

Be sure to have the slides on hand before you start the assembly of the drawers. Check the instructions to determine the required clearances. Most ball-bearing slides require about ½-inch clearance on each side, which means the overall width of the drawer will have to be reduced 1 inch. Some center-type guides call for the front-to-back depth of the drawer to be reduced by ½ inch or more—read the instructions.

Where possible, make all the drawers the same size. It will require only a little more time to make a dozen than to make one or two. This is not always possible, of course. Some base cabinets have drawers from top to bottom and require several sizes with the larger ones on the bottom.

With a little planning it is possible to make all the drawers above the doors in the base cabinet the same size. The fronts of some corner base cabinets, behind which a lazy-Susan is installed, sometimes are fitted with full-length doors and no drawers. That is, no drawer is fitted just under the counter-top. Your design will look more uniform if you make a "false" drawer on each door for such a corner cabinet.

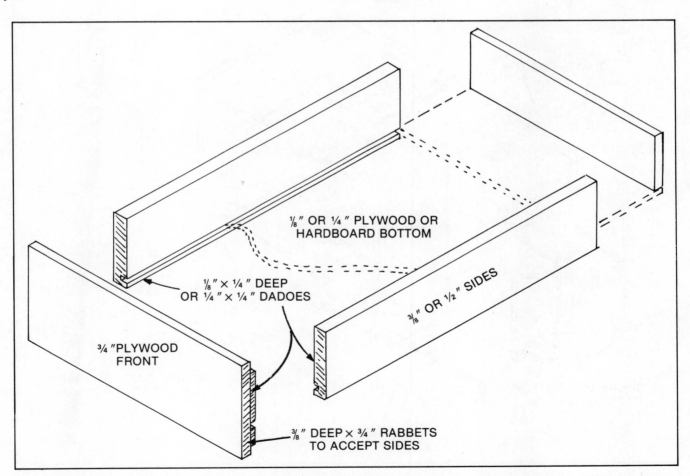

The standard method of making drawers for cabinets is detailed. The front and sides of the drawer are grooved to accept a bottom that "floats" in grooves. The drawer back sets on top of the bottom and is held with just a couple brads.

Corner Cabinets

When making a corner cabinet, the first decision is to determine what size it will be. The cabinet can be built to the full 24-inch depth, as the other cabinets adjacent to it, or it can be made shallower to conserve lumber and space. The largest circular shelves are 28 inches in diameter, and this will not quite fill the available space in the corner. Each door, however, would have to be made a full 18 inches wide for this larger circular shelf. Corner cabinets should not be very wide, because the space can be better utilized for regular cabinets.

Keeping cabinet doors 12 inches wide will allow using a 22- or 24-inch diameter shelf, and the cabinet will be a practical size. Build the cabinet to the dimensions specified in the illustration. Note that the top and bottom shelves are the same size and ¾ inch longer in both dimensions to allow for the ⅜-inch projections into the ⅜-inch dadoes cut in the sides at the bottom and the rabbets at the top.

Install the lazy-Susan hardware according to the instructions specified on the package. Glue and nail the facing strips of 1 x 2 stock, after carefully measuring. Both doors are the same height, but one is ¾ inch narrower than the other to allow for the ¾-inch thickness of the door in front. Doors are fastened directly to the angles in the notched shelves with wood screws.

Edges of the doors must be slightly beveled to permit their slipping past the front trim. You can purchase positioning stops to hold the doors in the closed position, so they will be flush with the rest of the cabinet doors.

Finish the toe space of the cabinet to match that of the other cabinets; this can be done after all the cabinets are installed. Note that the corner cabinet is screwed to the adjacent cabinets, or you can use nuts and bolts. Cleats are fastened to the wall near the corner to provide support for the cabinet top.

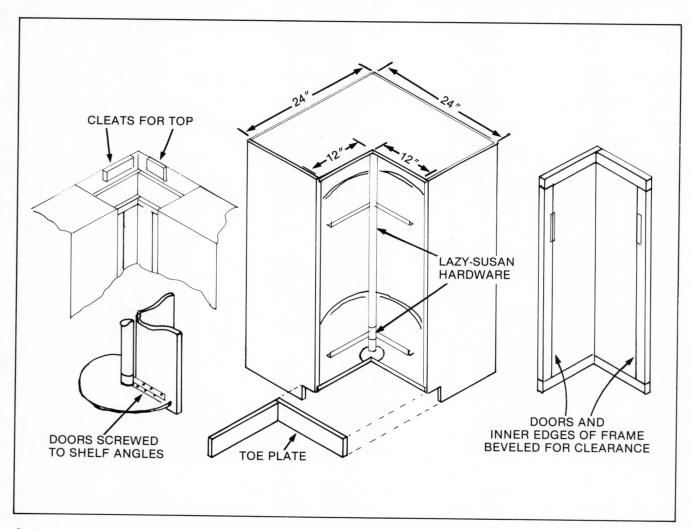

CLEATS FOR TOP

24" 24"

12" 12"

LAZY-SUSAN HARDWARE

DOORS SCREWED TO SHELF ANGLES

TOE PLATE

DOORS AND INNER EDGES OF FRAME BEVELED FOR CLEARANCE

Corner cabinets are fitted with a set of lazy-Susan shelves to utilize all storage space. Doors are kept to 12 inches wide, as wider cabinets would waste space. Hardware is available to permit making your own wooden shelves, or you can buy pre-made metal shelves with a cutout that fits corners.

Cabinet Installation

Proper cabinet installation is not difficult if patience and care are taken with the project. Precise measuring and leveling techniques will help eliminate many of the problems associated with cabinet installation. All houses and walls are different, and you may have to adjust your cabinets to conform with the conditions of your home. In most cases, proper leveling, measuring, and shimming will result in a professional-looking job.

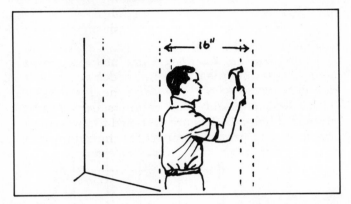

1—Cabinets must be attached to studs for full support. Studs are usually located 16 inches on center. Locate studs with a stud finder, tapping with hammer or nail driven through plaster at height that will be hidden by cabinets. Cabinets must always be attached to walls with screws. Never use nails.

2—Cabinets must be installed perfectly level—from a standpoint of function as well as appearance. Find the highest point of the floor with the use of a level.

3—Using a level or straightedge, find the high spots on the wall on which cabinets are to be hung. Some high spots can be removed by sanding. It may be necessary to shim to provide a level and plumb installation.

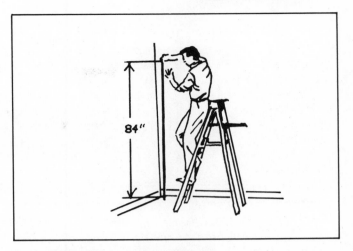

4—Using the highest point on the floor, measure up the wall to the height of 84 inches. This height is the top height of wall cabinets, oven, and broom cabinets.

5—On the walls where cabinets are to be installed, remove baseboard and chair rail. This is required for a flush fit.

6—Start your installation in one corner. First assemble the base corner unit, then add one unit on each side of the corner unit. This can be installed in position as a unit. Additional cabinets are then added to each side.

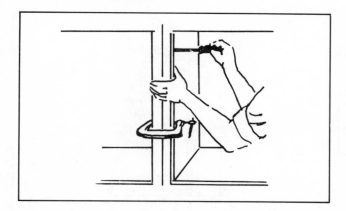

7—"C" clamps should be used in connecting cabinets together to obtain proper alignment. Drill 2 or 3 holes through the ½-inch end panels. Holes should be drilled through to the adjoining cabinet. Secure with a T-nut and a 1½-inch bolt. Draw up snugly.

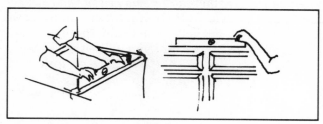

8—Each cabinet, as it is installed to the wall, should be checked front to back and also across the front edge with a level. Be certain that the front frame is plumb. If necessary, use shims to level the cabinets. Base cabinets should be attached with screws into wall studs. For additional support and to prevent the back rail from bowing, insert a block between the cabinet back and wall. After bases are installed and shimmed, cover toe kick area with material that is provided.

9—Attach the countertop on base cabinets. After installation, cover countertops with cartons to prevent damage while completing installation.

10—Wall cabinets should then be installed, beginning with a corner unit as described in step #6. Screw through hanging strips built into the backs of cabinets at both top and bottom. Place them ¾ inch below top and ¾ inch above bottom shelf from inside of cabinet. Adjust only loosely at first to permit final adjustments.

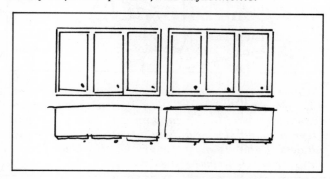

11—Wall cabinets should be checked with a level on cabinet front, sides, and bottom to ensure that cabinets are plumb and level. It might be necessary to shim at wall and between cabinets to correct for uneven walls or floors. After cabinets and doors are perfectly aligned, tighten all screws. Instructions courtesy of Kitchen Kompact

Bookcases and Shelves

Bookcases and bookshelves are basically built the same as cabinets, but usually need to be stronger because of the considerable weight of books. The styling differs from that of cabinets. You may have doors that conceal the lower shelves, but the upper shelves are usually open. Additionally, the lower cabinet must support not only the weight it contains, but also the top cabinet plus all the books and magazines it will hold.

Construction Tips

To strengthen the lower cabinet, include partitions spaced no more than 3 feet apart. A space less than 3 feet will not hold many books or other items, so you may want to reinforce the upper portion of the cabinet to permit a span of 3 feet or more.

This is done by using a facing 1 x 4 stock across the top of the base cabinet, rather than the usual 1 x 2. The facing then hides a 2 x 4 that is fitted across the top of the cabinet. It makes the cabinet more rigid and also supports the plywood top on which the upper bookcase rests.

The partitions are notched to fit around the 2 x 4s, one being located at the back and one at the front. A bookcase can be used either as a unit against the wall, or free-standing in a room to create a room divider.

If it is the latter, you might want doors on both sides of the lower cabinet, to provide access from both sides. By the same reasoning, you will want to make the open shelves at the top wide enough so books can be fitted on both sides, doubling the amount of shelf space.

Most hardback books are about 8½ inches high and about 6 inches wide. If you have a number of reference books, encyclopedias and the like, they will of course be bigger and you will either have to make wider shelves (deeper) or figure on inserting these larger books from only one side of your bookshelves. Where this is the case, it might be a better idea to apply paneling to the one side of the room divider, particularly if the room is paneled. If it is not, and there is wallpaper on the room walls, you can apply smooth hardboard to the back of the bookshelves and cover it with the wallpaper or wallcovering used on the room walls.

The base of the lower cabinet should be made of 2 x 4s also, to provide needed strength. The lumber is covered with strips of the hardwood-plywood used for the cabinet.

These bookshelves are combined with cabinets below. They are "architectural" in that they were built when the house was constructed and are styled to match the fireplace. Shelves are adjustable, with clips in holes in the side pieces.

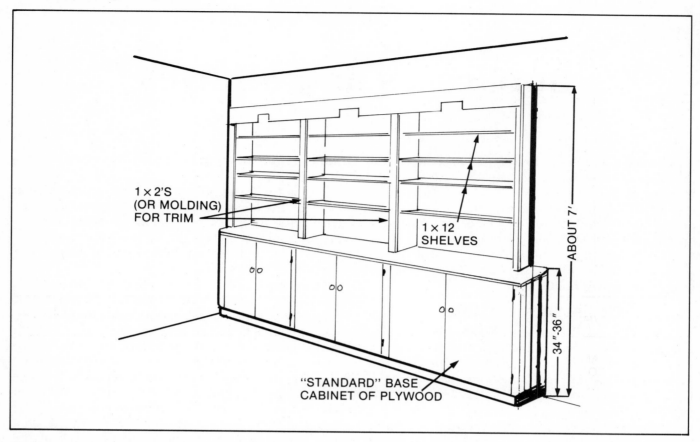

1 × 2'S
(OR MOLDING)
FOR TRIM

1 × 12
SHELVES

ABOUT 7'

34"-36"

"STANDARD" BASE
CABINET OF PLYWOOD

Many homes have recessed wall areas that are ideal for   built-in bookshelves.

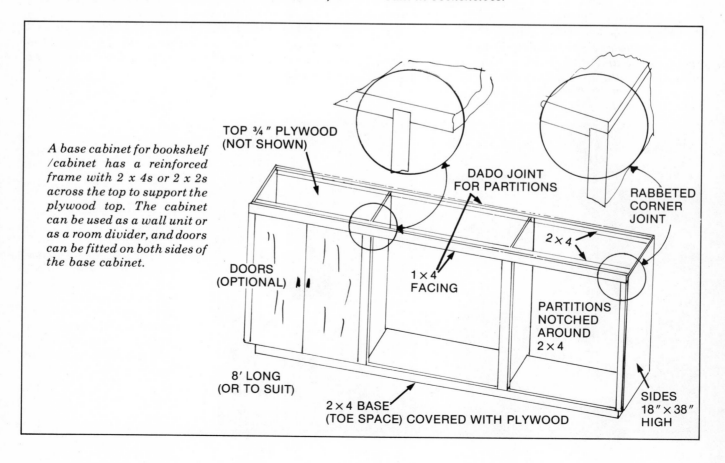

A base cabinet for bookshelf /cabinet has a reinforced frame with 2 x 4s or 2 x 2s across the top to support the plywood top. The cabinet can be used as a wall unit or as a room divider, and doors can be fitted on both sides of the base cabinet.

TOP ¾" PLYWOOD
(NOT SHOWN)

DADO JOINT
FOR PARTITIONS

RABBETED
CORNER
JOINT

2 × 4

DOORS
(OPTIONAL)

1 × 4
FACING

PARTITIONS
NOTCHED
AROUND
2 × 4

8' LONG
(OR TO SUIT)

2 × 4 BASE
(TOE SPACE) COVERED WITH PLYWOOD

SIDES
18" × 38"
HIGH

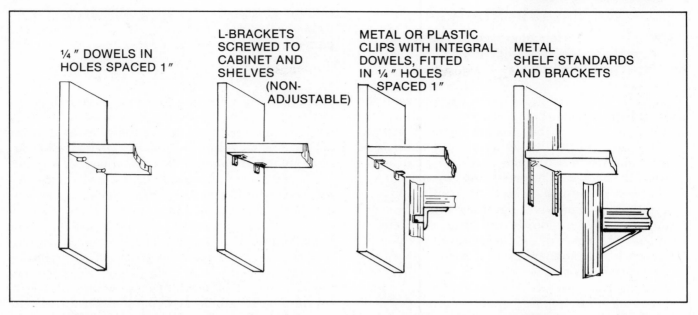

¼" DOWELS IN HOLES SPACED 1"

L-BRACKETS SCREWED TO CABINET AND SHELVES (NON-ADJUSTABLE)

METAL OR PLASTIC CLIPS WITH INTEGRAL DOWELS, FITTED IN ¼" HOLES SPACED 1"

METAL SHELF STANDARDS AND BRACKETS

Shelves can be fixed rigidly in dadoes, or with metal   *angle brackets, or made adjustable by several devices.*

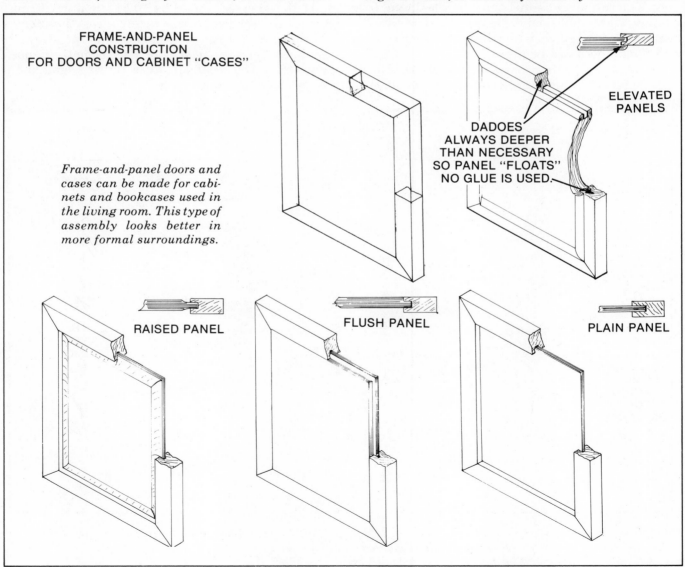

FRAME-AND-PANEL CONSTRUCTION FOR DOORS AND CABINET "CASES"

Frame-and-panel doors and cases can be made for cabinets and bookcases used in the living room. This type of assembly looks better in more formal surroundings.

DADOES ALWAYS DEEPER THAN NECESSARY SO PANEL "FLOATS" NO GLUE IS USED.

ELEVATED PANELS

RAISED PANEL

FLUSH PANEL

PLAIN PANEL

Adjustable Shelves

If you have a variety of sizes of books, it's a good idea to make the shelves adjustable. They then can be spaced to accept any size of books you have.

There are a number of ways this can be done. First, drill a series of holes in the side pieces of the cabinet in which short lengths of wooden dowel are inserted to support the shelves. Space the holes about 1 inch apart. The same kind of spacing of holes is done for metal or plastic clips you can buy to support the shelves. The projecting dowel portion of the clips is ¼ inch, so make the holes that size.

A bit more expensive, but very attractive and strong, are shelf standards into which brackets are snapped. The spacing for these standards is a bit less than 1 inch, so they can be adjusted to any size book or decorative item.

Because bookcases or bookshelves will be in a living room or other more formal room, doors will be more decorative than those used for kitchen cabinets. The frame-and-panel type are good, and four examples are shown in cross section. The rails, of course, are solid stock, while the panels for the plain and flush doors can be plywood.

Stock for projecting or raised panels should be solid lumber, either hardwood or softwood. The sides and backs of the cabinets that have been made as bookcases or bookshelves also can be frame and panel.

Simple Shelves

The most common bookcase or bookshelf is one assembled from straight-grained pine shelving which is installed, then painted or stained. Painting is the usual way that shelves are finished if they are to be installed as an architectural part of a room.

When we say "architectural," we mean quite literally that the shelves are part of the basic structure of the room. A recess in a room or a niche, say alongside a fireplace, is a common location for such bookshelves or bookcases. The shelves can be supported by any of the devices previously described, if the vertical members of the assembly are wood. The devices cannot be used, of course, in a plaster or plasterboard wall, because these materials will not support much weight.

If the shelves are to be fixed, then cut dadoes across the vertical members and insert the shelves. In the case of a recess or niche, build the assembly so that when the shelves are inserted in the dadoes, they force the vertical pieces tightly against the sides of the recess or niche.

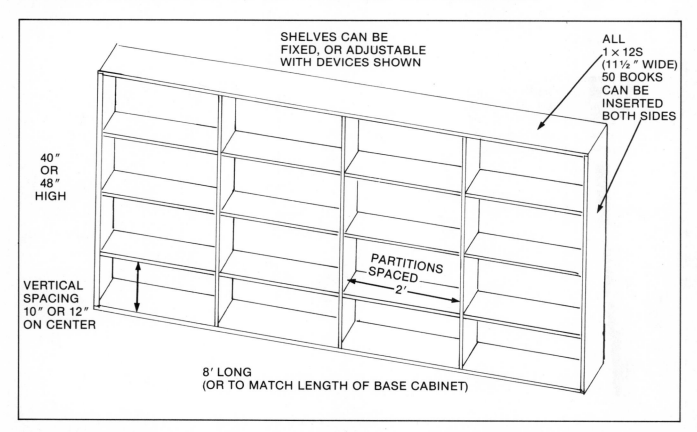

Simple shelving is made to rest on a base cabinet, and it also can be used as a wall unit or room divider. If used as a wall unit, shelves could be 1 x 8s or 1 x 10s; shelves shown would allow a standard book to be inserted on both sides.

Shelves installed by the homeowner have an architectural look, as they were assembled in a recess in the wall, then painted to match the wall. Shelves are cut from plain pine shelving. Photo courtesy of Armstrong Cork Co.

These kitchen cabinets look elaborate but they are quite simple. The corner cabinet helps the kitchen turn the corner without creating dead space. Photo courtesy of Quaker Maid

Specialty Shelves

If you can only locate the bookcase in a corner of the room, you can try a corner cabinet, although the shape of such a cabinet does not really lend itself to holding books. One answer to the corner cabinet is to utilize bookends at the end of each row of books, then place some kind of decorative item beside each bookend adjacent to the slanting or angled side of the case.

Where space is even more restricted, you might consider a small bookcase that doubles as an end table. Where only a few books are to be made available, you can have one or two shelves in a chairside bookcase, with a storage cabinet beneath for paperback books and magazines.

Another corner possibility is a corner seat with a window shelf. Use a bright and cheerful wallcovering on the upper walls, a matching fabric on the cushions of the built-in seat, and a contrasting wallcovering on the lower part of the built-in. Molding adds a nice touch. There are lift-up plywood covers that conceal all kinds of storage beneath the cushions.

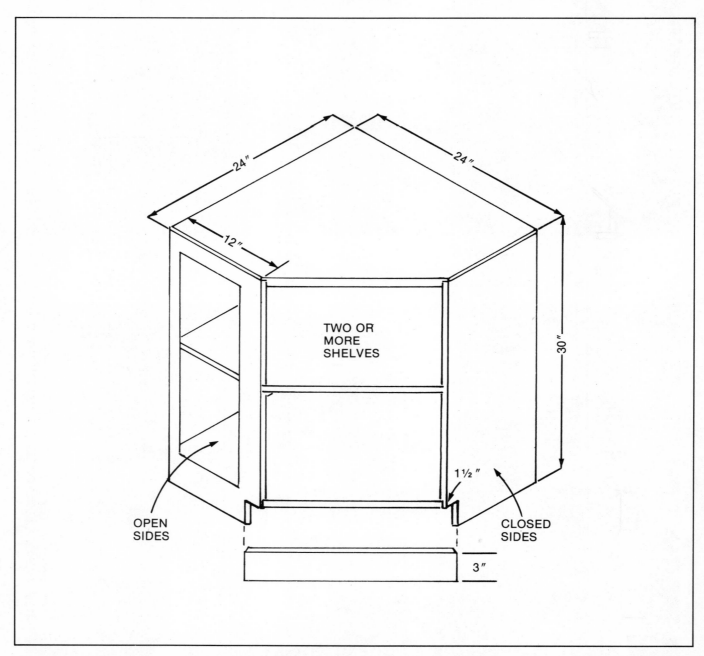

A corner cabinet can be table or desk height. A closed cabinet, as shown on the right side, is not handy for books. The left half of cabinet has open construction.

More shelves can be installed, of course. This cabinet can be made square for chairside use.

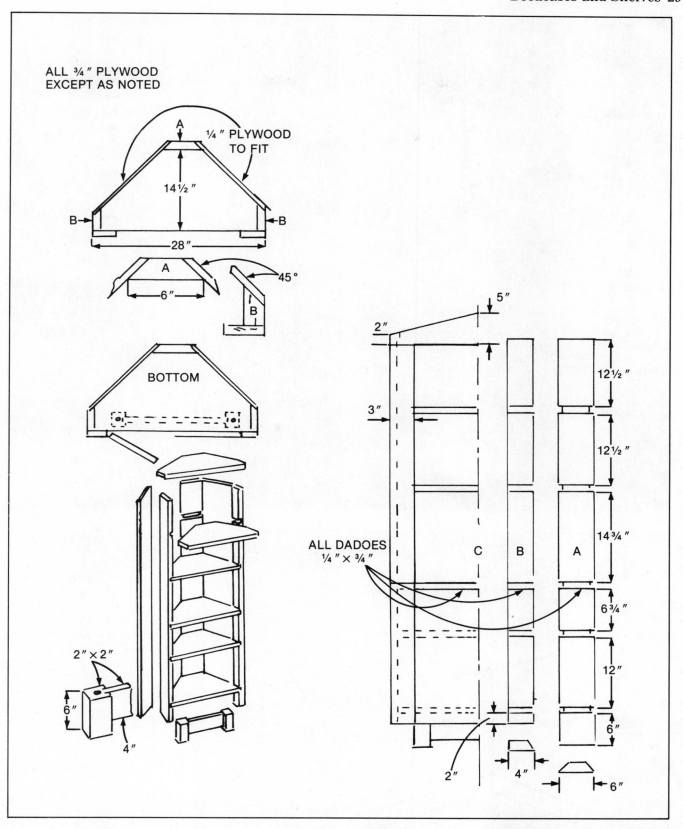

ALL ¾" PLYWOOD
EXCEPT AS NOTED

¼" PLYWOOD
TO FIT

14½"

28"

A

6"

45°

B

BOTTOM

2" × 2"

6"

4"

2"

5"

3"

ALL DADOES
¼" × ¾"

C   B   A

12½"

12½"

14¾"

6¾"

12"

6"

2"

4"

6"

A corner cabinet can utilize space in a corner of the room, but this is not too handy for books. This cabinet has pieces "A" and "B" cut from ¾-inch plywood or 1-inch solid stock, then dadoes as indicated. All shelves are cut to the same size; all angles are 45 degrees at the back and edge. The trim can be shaped to suit, as can the pediment at top—shown with triangular shape. Pieces of ¼-inch plywood are cut to fit between "A" and "B" pieces after shelves are fitted in dadoes. You can install doors on the lower part of the cabinet or eliminate them.

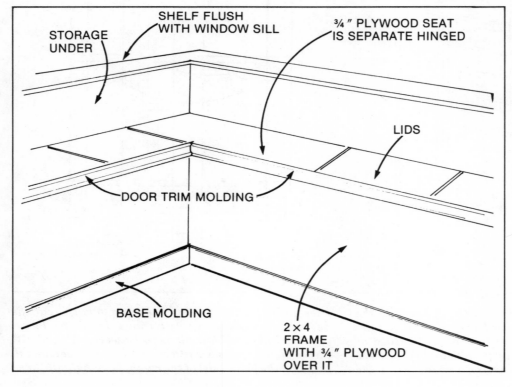

STORAGE
UNDER

SHELF FLUSH
WITH WINDOW SILL

¾" PLYWOOD SEAT
IS SEPARATE HINGED

LIDS

DOOR TRIM MOLDING

BASE MOLDING

2 × 4
FRAME
WITH ¾" PLYWOOD
OVER IT

You can fill more than one need by using this plan. This L-shaped bench hides plenty of usable storage space and could be adapted to any room in the house. The matching wallpaper and fabric make it appear built-in.

This simple bookshelf, built in a niche against a living room wall, can be ordinary pine shelving of 1 x 6, 1 x 8, 1 x 10, or 1 x 12 stock. For shelves of added thickness, without great increase in weight, shelves can be assembled from framing of 1 x 2s with ⅛- or ¼-inch hardboard glued and bradded to both sides. Shelves are painted to match the wall. Note that the bottom shelf on each end of the bookcase is flush with the top of the table at the end of the sofa. The center section of the bookcase is raised to create a frame for the sofa and to provide display area for photographs and paintings.

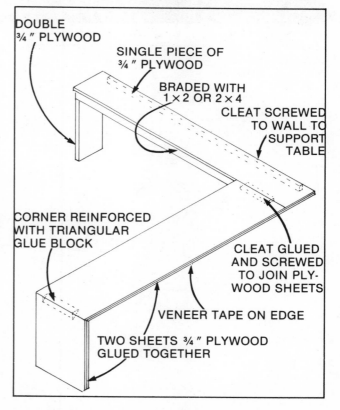

The simple decor of this room calls for simple built-ins. The table behind the couch extends in an L-shape to become a large shelf for plants and a television set. Photo courtesy of Tile Council of America

Even a very modern and glamorous living room needs built-ins. This room has storage under and behind the seats as well as in the cabinets, drawers, and bookshelves above the seats. Photo courtesy of Tile Council of America

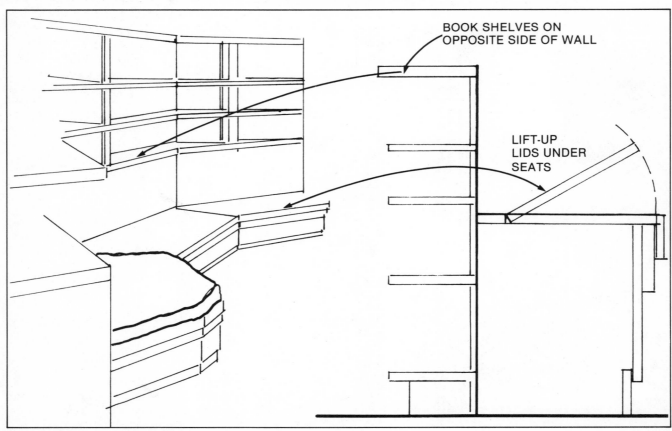

BOOK SHELVES ON
OPPOSITE SIDE OF WALL

LIFT-UP
LIDS UNDER
SEATS

Wall systems such as these are ideal for creating a focus wall and providing storage at the same time. You can choose enclosed or open modules to suit your own needs. Elegant furniture balances the heft of the wall unit. Photo courtesy of Armstrong Cork

This bright kitchen has very ample storage space despite its small size. All appliances and various utensils have a spot in this highly organized kitchen. Photo courtesy of Armstrong Cork

A colorfully painted cabinet wall holds all the accessories needed for indoor gardening. Although the units are freestanding, they have a built-in look. Alternating white and yellow sections make it easy to remember what is stored in each area. Photo courtesy of Ethan Allen

Attractive wall shelving units are possible using simple pine boards. See the chapter on Bookcases and Shelves for instructions on how to build this unit.

The design idea of integrating rooms with cabinetry is shown in this oak kitchen-dining room combination. More and more kitchen cabinet units are being used in other rooms of the house. Photo courtesy of Coppes

Don't be afraid to aim for a great kitchen. You might not have space for this one (above left), but it can be scaled down. These are stock cabinets that come in modular sizes so they can be fitted into any room. Photo courtesy of IXL

Painted cabinets in this kitchen (left) have flush doors and drawer fronts to present a smooth uniform surface. Photo courtesy of Armstrong Cork

Cabinet framing is stained a light color to match the paneling on the walls, while doors and drawer fronts are made from darker-stained hardwood-plywood for contrast. Photo courtesy of Armstrong Cork

This spacious kitchen utilizes corner space with a built-in range unit. Ample counter space on either side of the range creates a very efficient working area. Photo courtesy of SK Advertising

Softwood plywood was used to create this arched wall (upper right) and to decorate the rest of the interior with the warmth of wood. Note how this F-1-Yer included built-in storage walls. Photo courtesy of American Plywood Assn.

The modern look of these cabinets (lower right) was created with a stenciled pattern that duplicated the painted design on each door. Note how the design is repeated in the adjacent room in the wall covering and a hanging decorator piece. Photo courtesy of Armstrong Cork

Flush doors in these kitchen cabinets have arched openings with cloth inserts supported by a metal grille. The rabbet on the back side of the opening permits securing of both cloth and grille. Photo courtesy of Armstrong Cork

This entertainment center was made with cabinets, all of which are standard units. Framing members and top arches can be constructed by the owner or a carpenter, and the countertops can be custom-made by a plastic fabricator. Photo courtesy of IXL

Standard kitchen cabinets were used to finish off this room, giving ample storage space for entertaining. Photo courtesy of Boise Cascade

This wall unit serves as a home entertainment center in this family room. Plastic laminate countertops and shelves contrast nicely with the richly colored wood cabinet doors. Photo courtesy of Georgia Pacific

Simple shelving units flank this built-in desk top. The pine shelving exhibits various sculptures and books. Photo courtesy of American Plywood Assn.

This sewing center in a cabinet has two roll out sections (above right). One for the sewing machine has two lift-up leaves. Drawers in the supply cabinet have dividers to organize supplies and materials. When not arranged for sewing, shutters close the center. Reprinted by permission of Woman's Day magazine © 1976 by Fawcett Publications, Inc.

An ingenious sewing center becomes a beautiful armoire when closed. The working surface for the sewing machine slides out of a separate table, which pivots in front of the tall piece. Photo courtesy of Edmund D. Motyka

Bookshelves on the wall of this room are a simple assembly of pine shelving stock. Metal brackets are screwed to vertical partitions to hold metal clips that support shelves at the desired spacing. The lamp table is a plywood box to which paneling is adhered. A glass top completes the table, which can be readily disassembled for moving. Photo courtesy of Z-Brick Co.

Adjustable shelves (above right) supported on wall brackets extend in front of the window, where they hold plants and other room accessories. The modern table desk is made of a door on metal supports and contrasts in mood with the Oriental rug. Photo courtesy of Edmund D Motyka

Everything is right at hand and all in order for this functional activity room (lower right). A multitude of hobbies can be organized with open storage such as this. Colorful carpeting acts as the unifying agent; it is actually easily installed carpet tiles. Photo courtesy of Armstrong Cork

Handsome, dark built-in bookshelves greatly enhance the decor of this den. Photo courtesy of Vermont Weatherboard

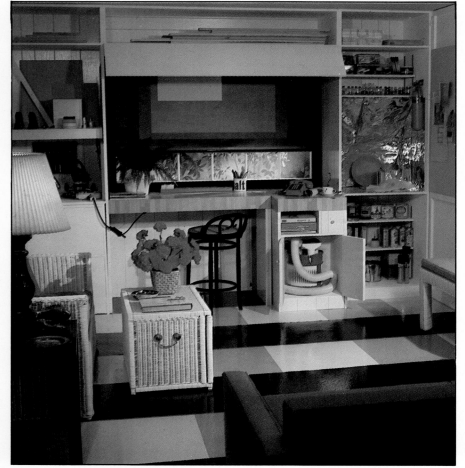

The use of kitchen cabinets to furnish other rooms of the house is shown here, with standard cabinets supplemented by furniture pieces made for furniture groupings. Photo courtesy of Overton

You do not have to live in an Early American house to have a traditional family room (upper right). Stucco overhead beams, a built-in shelving unit, paneling, homespun fabrics, and warm accessories set the tone. Photo courtesy of Barcalounger Recliners

Gourmets can store extra cooking aids in the surrounding cabinet units in this combination family room and kitchen (lower right). Straw baskets and a natural fiber rug contribute to the country look of the furnishings. Photo courtesy of Ethan Allen

This guest room doubles as a home workshop for the handyman. Cabinets are built out from the window wall. The butcher block table at the window serves as a workbench and was used to make the cabinetry in the room. The cabinetry at left opens to reveal various tools. Shallow cabinets along the ceiling hold lumber of various sizes. Photo courtesy of Edmund D. Motyka

This attic bathroom utilizes standard cabinet and vanity units for storage of towels and toiletries. Photo courtesy of SK Advertising

This built-in bathroom vanity features a laminate countertop and an under-the-counter lavatory basin. The wood used in the vanity matches the paneling. Photo courtesy of Aster

Storage Everywhere

There are literally hundreds of cubic feet of storage space in every home that is completely overlooked. Storage inside interior walls and partitions is only a few inches deep, but it is absolutely ideal for canned goods, bottled products, paper towels, and other small items.

Storage Walls

Some kitchens will have wall space that can be utilized for storing food, and very often the walls of a stairway provide another out-of-the-way location for a wall pantry.

In the example shown, a hallway was converted to a storage area, after the owners decided to panel the walls; this was to be the initial step in creating a "pantry."

First, cover the floor with several layers of newspaper to protect it from falling plaster. Next, hammer a few holes in the wall, being careful not to hit any pipes or wires. If there is baseboard molding at the floor, remove it.

Use a level to mark a horizontal line on the wall (or walls) about 5 inches below the ceiling. Score across this line with a linoleum or utility knife. This will be the top of your wall pantry; the ends of the line should be just inside the two studs that will be the ends of your pantry. Set the level vertical, after you have knocked holes in the wall to determine the position of the top and bottom of each end stud, and mark along the wall to indicate where the studs are. Score along the two vertical lines, then break out all the plaster or plasterboard between the two vertical and the horizontal lines, down to the floor. You now have a series of exposed 2 x 4 studs, the backs of which are covered with the plasterboard on the opposite side. If wires or pipes are exposed, build a box around them. You don't want canned goods abrading the insulation on wiring or banging on pipe connections to cause possible leaks.

Next, measure the thickness of the plasterboard and shim out the face of each stud by that thickness. Interior plasterboard generally is ⅜ inch, but could be ½ inch. Old-fashioned plaster can vary considerably. Make each open stud flush with the surface of the wall you have opened.

Measure from the back of each stud opening to the face of the shims. This length will be approximately 4 inches. Cut cleats of light material, say ½ x 1 inch. The spacing of the cleats and shelves will depend on the sizes of the items stored. Start from the floor and set packages or cans in place, then space the next shelf up to allow about ¼ inch above the first row of items. Glue and nail the cleats.

Shelves can be ½-inch stock or plywood. Don't fasten the shelves; simply slip them onto the cleats.

A paneled hallway actually is a pantry with shelves for canned goods, paper towels, detergent containers, etc., that require dozens of shelves. Except for hinges, there is no sign of the hidden cabinets.

After plasterboard is removed, you may find wiring or plumbing that will have to be boxed in to protect it. The large mass shown is a plaster-soaked excelsior to hold a fixture in the bathroom on the opposite side of the wall.

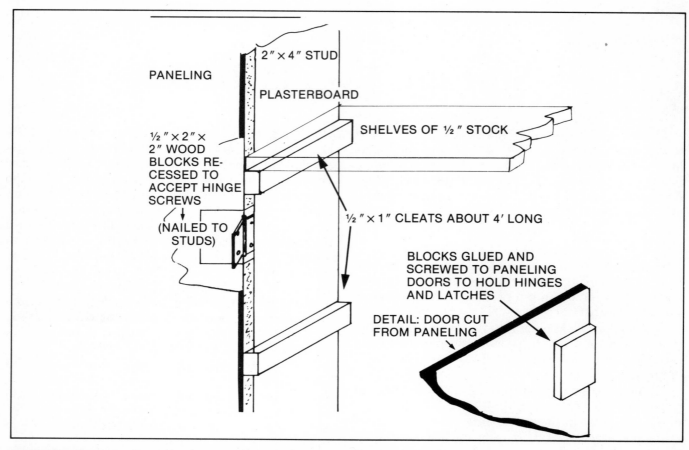

PANELING

2″ × 4″ STUD

PLASTERBOARD

½″ × 2″ × 2″ WOOD BLOCKS RECESSED TO ACCEPT HINGE SCREWS

(NAILED TO STUDS)

SHELVES OF ½″ STOCK

½″ × 1″ CLEATS ABOUT 4′ LONG

BLOCKS GLUED AND SCREWED TO PANELING DOORS TO HOLD HINGES AND LATCHES

DETAIL: DOOR CUT FROM PANELING

Shelves are spaced by actually setting various sizes of food tins on each one, then spacing next shelf about ¼ inch higher for clearance. Here shelves are spaced for small and large food tins.

Shelf cleats are cut from ½-inch stock, and glued and nailed to 2 x 4 studs in wall. Shelves are left loose so they can be removed for storage of items that are quite tall.

This makes it possible to remove a shelf when taller items are to be stored on a shelf.

After the shelves and cleats have been positioned, remove the shelves so you can paint the inside of the "pantry," painting the back of the plasterboard, the 2 x 4 studs, and the shelves. The next step is the paneling.

Apply the paneling with panel adhesive from a caulking gun. Cartridges of the adhesive are sold in most hardware stores and home centers. A nail gun helps speed the job, and there now are electric-powered nail guns on the market. They speed the job even more and eliminate the fatigue that used to result from the manual nail guns with their heavy springs.

Cut the paneling at the beginning of the "pantry" and at the end. In between, cut the doors so they have their edges on 2 x 4s, and the tops and bottoms are on the center line of shelves. Note that it was necessary to glue and screw blocks to the insides of the doors to accept the hinge and latch screws. Blocks also are recessed into the plaster at the end studs. Touch-type latches were used, requiring only a push on the door to open and close it. All that is visible on the "pantry" wall are the backs of the

The door for a cassette cabinet overlaps the opening a couple of inches all around. The inside was painted bright red with a gloss paint.

Because paneling is only ¼ inch thick, blocks of ½-inch stock are glued and bradded to inside of panel doors to hold hinge screws and attach latch part of touch-type latches.

A small door is cut in the wall to hold cassette tapes. Hinges used here are the plastic type without pins. Hinges later were painted to match the paneling so they were less noticeable.

This cabinet is a built-in, utilizing wallpaper to match the surrounding walls. The molding treatment helps draw the eye to the books and artifacts. Photo courtesy of Wallcovering Industry Bureau, United-DeSoto

The wall with the cassette cabinet also had a broom closet, light switch and thermostat. Trim around the door has been removed here. The next step was to cut the floor of the cabinet flush with the surface of the plasterboard. The base molding here also was removed before paneling was applied. After paneling was applied, with the light-switch cover and thermostat replaced, the closet door is almost invisible.

hinges, which can be painted to match the paneling.

Only one wall of the hall shown was used as a pantry; on the opposite wall a small cabinet was made to store tape cassettes. On the same wall there was a broom closet. To conceal the closet, the trim was removed from around the door and the paneling was run to the edges of the opening. The door then was covered with paneling and seemed to disappear.

To finish the job, the shoe molding (quarter-round) was replaced, but not the baseboard. This

An open stairway with treads but no risers is typical of many basements. Steel beams alongside the stairway have to be enclosed with framework, then covered with paneling or plasterboard.

was a decision by the homeowner. Another builder might prefer to use new molding.

Stairway Storage

Stairways are another storage area that often is overlooked. When a basement is remodeled for living space, the stairs are simply painted or carpeted and considered only as a way to get from one floor to another.

Many basement stairs are simple wooden structures consisting of stringers with treads, but no risers. If you intend to install risers on this type of stairway, why not make them small doors that open to a series of small but handy cabinets?

Shelves to create the bottoms of the small cabinets can be glued and nailed to the underside of the next lower tread, then boxed-in on the sides and back.

A bit more complicated is the arrangement where vertical "dividers" are nailed to the back edges of the treads; each divider is of a length that brings it flush with the edges of the stringer. A sheet of plywood is nailed to the back edges of the risers to create a series of boxes with slanting bottoms. You might want to cut the bottom edges of the dividers at an angle to make them fit snugly against the plywood backing. With a bit of measuring you could determine where to nail through the plywood into the lower edges of the dividers. Drop-down doors would be most practical, but side-hinged doors also could be utilized.

The space under the stairs is another potential storage area, and it is much more apparent in most cases. You could combine the step cabinets with such a closet.

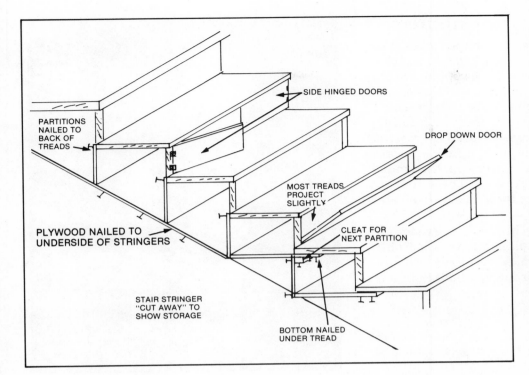

SIDE HINGED DOORS

PARTITIONS NAILED TO BACK OF TREADS

DROP DOWN DOOR

MOST TREADS PROJECT SLIGHTLY

PLYWOOD NAILED TO UNDERSIDE OF STRINGERS

CLEAT FOR NEXT PARTITION

STAIR STRINGER "CUT AWAY" TO SHOW STORAGE

BOTTOM NAILED UNDER TREAD

Open risers of a stairway can be made into doors that permit reaching into one of two types of small cabinets built under the stairs. One type is created by nailing a sheet of plywood to the underside of stringers, then nailing vertical partitions to the back edges of treads. You actually would install partitions first, determining their size by holding a straightedge across the underside of the stringers. The second type is made by nailing one piece under the tread and a second piece on the back edge of the tread. Additional vertical pieces would require a 1 x 1-inch cleat as indicated.

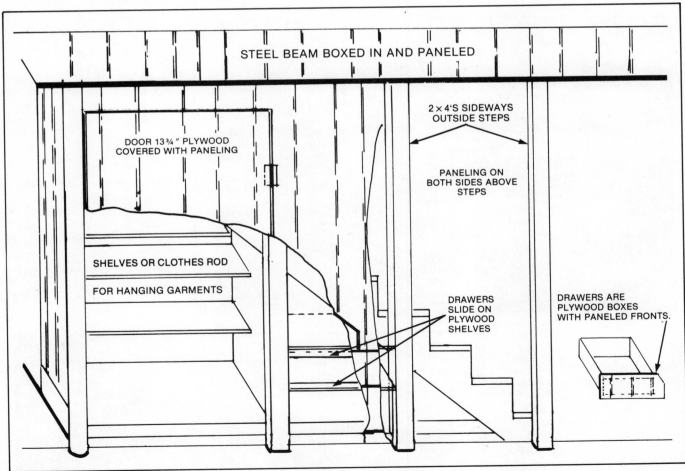

STEEL BEAM BOXED IN AND PANELED

DOOR 13¾" PLYWOOD COVERED WITH PANELING

2 x 4'S SIDEWAYS OUTSIDE STEPS

PANELING ON BOTH SIDES ABOVE STEPS

SHELVES OR CLOTHES ROD

FOR HANGING GARMENTS

DRAWERS SLIDE ON PLYWOOD SHELVES

DRAWERS ARE PLYWOOD BOXES WITH PANELED FRONTS.

Step cabinets could be combined with a closet built under the stairway using shelves and/or a clothespole. Shorter space near the lower end of the stairway could be used for drawers; some could have odd-shaped fronts to match the angle of the steps.

Using Paneling for Cabinets

If you are building cabinets in a room that is to be paneled, the paneling can be used as a construction material. A simple framing of 2 x 4s can be used to support the lightweight paneling, and doors can be made by making frames of 1 x 2 stock. Drawers are framed of lighter stock inside the heavier framing, and simple guides assure easy working drawers. For an absolute match of the paneling, cut a piece to fit completely over the cabinet framing, then make cutouts for the doors and drawers. The saw kerfs provide necessary clearance for both the doors and drawers.

For the rustic look of wood in your living room, try embossed hardboard wall paneling. It is not only great for walls, whether applied vertically or diagonally, but can also be applied to any built-in that is constructed of solid lumber framing.

This impressive bar is a framing of 2 x 4s covered with the same paneling used for the walls. Paneling also covers the exposed studs in the wall and is cut into shallow arches above the bar.

Here, one piece of paneling is cut to fit the face of the cabinet, then cutouts are made for doors and drawers. Even if some cuts are a bit irregular, the cutouts match the openings exactly.

Doors are assembled from 1 x 2s, covered with paneling, and hung with plain butt hinges. Matching hardware used on the drawers is bolted through fronts. Note that the "drawer" in front of the sink actually is a tilt-down bin.

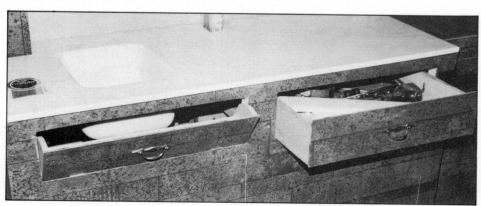

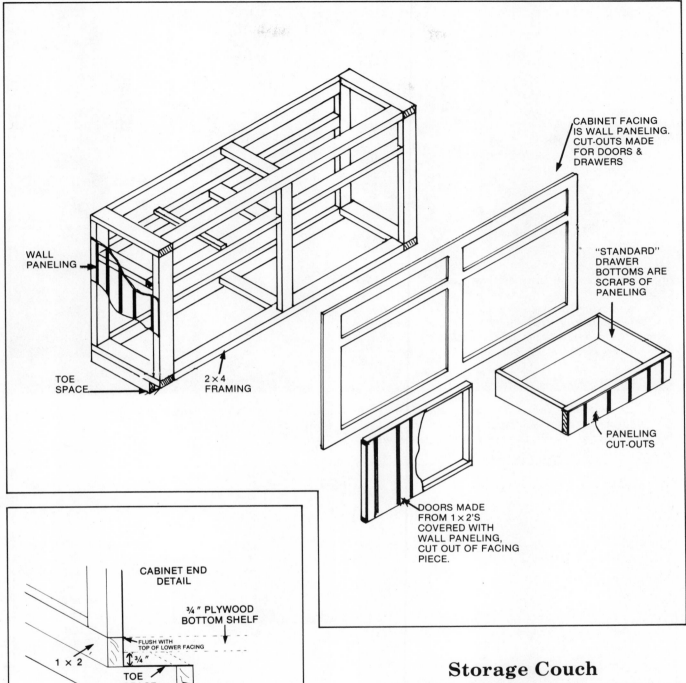

WALL
PANELING

TOE
SPACE

2 × 4
FRAMING

CABINET FACING
IS WALL PANELING.
CUT-OUTS MADE
FOR DOORS &
DRAWERS

"STANDARD"
DRAWER
BOTTOMS ARE
SCRAPS OF
PANELING

PANELING
CUT-OUTS

DOORS MADE
FROM 1 × 2'S
COVERED WITH
WALL PANELING,
CUT OUT OF FACING
PIECE.

CABINET END
DETAIL

¾" PLYWOOD
BOTTOM SHELF

FLUSH WITH
TOP OF LOWER FACING

¾"

1 × 2

TOE
SPACE
NOTCH

1 × 4 FACING
OF TOE-SPACE

Paneling covers the frame of rough 2 x 4s spiked together. Doors are frames of 1 x 2 stock covered inside and out with wall paneling. The front of the cabinet is one piece of paneling with cutouts made for doors and drawers.

Storage Couch

Like many built-ins, the couch is basically a box made by spiking together 2 x 4s for the main frame, then covering it with wall paneling. The seat of the couch is made of plywood that can be hinged to expose hidden storage beneath. Foam-rubber cushions or a foam-rubber mattress covered with upholstery material placed on the plywood base allows comfortable seating on top of the hidden storage space. An added touch is a shelf around the top of the couch, covered with ceramic tile. The shelf is a convenient place for beverages and is easily cleaned with a damp cloth. You now have a couch, counter, and storage cabinet in one easy-to-build unit.

Paneling, matching fabric, molding, and ceramic tile are combined in this corner built-in that creates a cheerful seating area. There is ample storage in compart- *ments below. Photo courtesy of Wallcovering Industry Bureau, Christopher Prints*

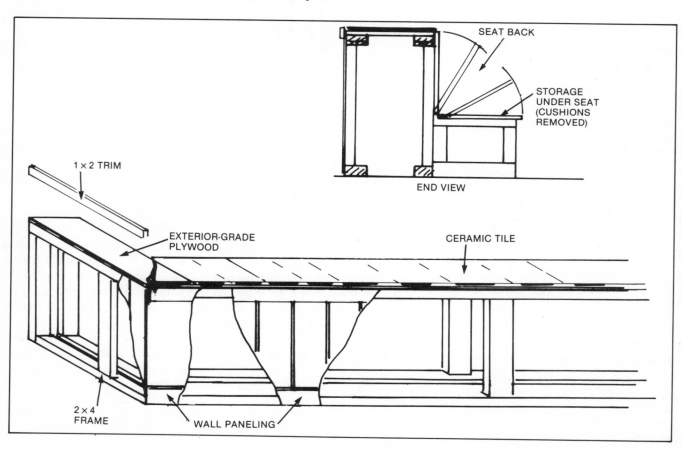

SEAT BACK

STORAGE
UNDER SEAT
(CUSHIONS
REMOVED)

END VIEW

1 × 2 TRIM

EXTERIOR-GRADE
PLYWOOD

CERAMIC TILE

2 × 4
FRAME

WALL PANELING

"Secret" panels are actually doors cut from plywood, trimmed with molding, inside of which wallcovering material is applied. Floor space is obtained by building a wall out from the original wall alongside the fireplace. Photo courtesy of Western Wood Moulding and Millwork Producers

Fireplace Footage

If you are going to do a remodeling job in a living room, family room, or basement, you can create secret panels and provide storage for all kinds of items by building a large cabinet from floor to ceiling. It can be only a few inches deep or as deep as you wish. Where there is a fireplace that extends into the room, the cabinet can be built flush with the face of the fireplace surround, or perhaps a few inches in back of it.

In the photo examples shown, plywood has been used for the cabinet, and the doors are pieces of the same ¾-inch plywood. Each door has been trimmed with molding and wallpaper, or a wallcovering material applied inside the molding. To make hidden cabinets, similar molded panels are located on other walls in the room.

The decor is colonial so the lower portions of the walls have a wainscot of paneling that is painted. The same kind of secret doors are installed in the wainscot. Shallow cabinets could be created, similar to the wall pantry on regular walls, using the molded-panel door idea.

There is a wide variety of stock moldings available, and you may combine several molding shapes to create your own individual molding. The molding should not be too heavy in a small room; conversely, very thin or lightweight molding would look out of place in a larger room.

Touch-type latches would be ideal for the doors over the secret compartments, but some provision should be made to minimize finger and handprints. You might consider a coat of clear flat varnish to prevent the paint from being smudged. The varnish also would make it easy to clean.

Panels on new wall match those on the exterior wall, but there are no "secret" cabinets behind the panels on the outside wall. Photo courtesy of Western Wood Moulding and Millwork Producers

Close-up of cabinets with doors open show that they are simply plywood boxes. Metal brackets are fitted on cabinet sides to permit adjusting shelves to any height desired. There also are "secret" panels on the lower wall below the chair rail. These smaller doors are trimmed with molding, but are painted rather than papered. Photo courtesy of Western Wood Moulding and Millwork Producers

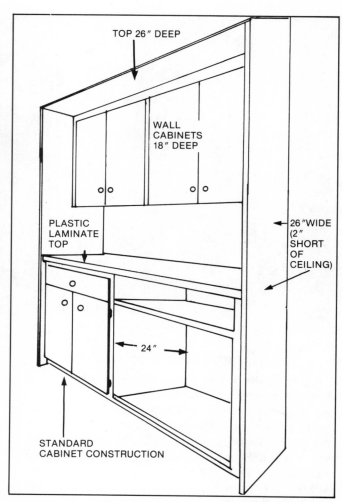

TOP 26″ DEEP

WALL CABINETS 18″ DEEP

PLASTIC LAMINATE TOP

26″ WIDE (2″ SHORT OF CEILING)

24″

STANDARD CABINET CONSTRUCTION

In a large kitchen, one end can be partitioned off with a room divider that runs from floor to ceiling. An ironing board can be hidden behind it; generous cabinets and drawers provide storage. The counter is used for folding clothes and other tasks. The room divider is basically a large, free-standing base and wall cabinet similar to those built in the kitchen. The sides and top of the divider are 2 inches wider than the cabinet, so the cabinet is not readily visible from the sides.

In this basement sewing room, mirrors are attached to hinged plywood panels so they can close face-to-face, with only the wall panels showing. The drop-down table is ¾-inch plywood, trimmed with molding and covered with wall paneling. Photo courtesy of Masonite Corporation

A ready-made corner cabinet creates a handy "built-in," but can be taken with you to another home. Finished or unfinished cabinets of this type are not too expensive and require little carpentry work. It may be necessary to notch the back edges of the cabinet to fit over existing molding. The shelf on the wall near the ceiling must remain, but is a handy and unique "built-in." The shelf provides a storage and display area for china and other items. The underside of the shelf is fitted with hooks to hang mugs or plants.

Molding nailed to the studs supports the shelf along the wall. Further support is provided by wooden brackets nailed on either side of the window trim, and to the studs at convenient locations. The railing is assembled from ready-made wooden spindles that are fitted in holes spaced equidistant in the top surface of the shelf and in spaced holes in a ¾ x ¾-inch strip that is the top rail of the gallery. Photo courtesy of Western Wood Moulding and Millwork Producers

Sewing Crannies

Don't overlook the sewing machine when you are remodeling upstairs, in the attic, or in the basement. There should be a place on one of these levels for a functional sewing room.

Cabinets should be floor-to-ceiling, carried out with the same steps as for the storage wall discussed early in the chapter. Bifold doors will make the sewing machine and cutting table readily accessible, yet completely hidden when not in use. An added touch is a three-panel mirror that is ideal for fitting and adjusting garments. In the arrangement shown, the two smaller side mirrors close on the larger one to completely disappear. The backs of the pivoting mirrors are covered with paneling to match the rest of the room.

Bonus Surfaces

If you build a handy work surface that can be used for hobbies and games, make it an inch or two off the floor and then build tables that slide under it. When there is a group or party in the house, the extra tables will really be useful. When not needed, they slide under the work counter and are completely out of the way.

Finally, be aware that most closets are extremely inefficient. You usually have one hanger rod or pole about 5 feet off the floor, with perhaps a shelf above that you can barely reach. There may be space on the floor for shoes and odds and ends, but never enough. Investigate the modern hardware, shelving and devices now available that can organize a closet.

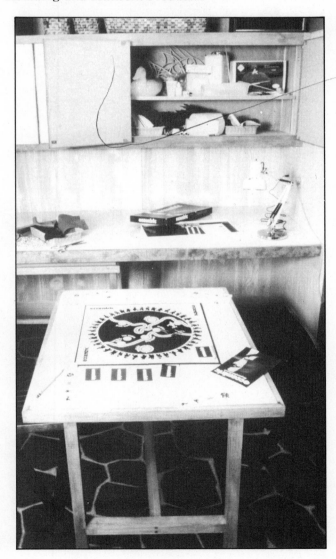

Making your work counter a couple inches higher than usual allows storage of a spare table underneath—useful for additional working space or for serving guests.

Bathroom Cabinets and Vanities

Bathroom cabinets are similar to those used in kitchens. The primary difference is what is stored. Rather than dishes and food, towels, washcloths, soap, and other bathroom needs are handled.

Because a bathroom is somewhat smaller than a kitchen, it takes less time and money to remodel it. Which means that you can "let yourself go" with the cabinets and the wallcovering to create a truly luxurious area. But since there is less space, careful planning for efficient storage space is necessary.

The various photos in this chapter show a number of different decorating schemes, but all are basically vanity cabinets (the base cabinet that contains the wash basin), plus floor and wallcoverings that are water-resistant and attractive.

Bathrooms vary so much in size and shape that it

Good-sized knobs are used as pulls on the doors and drawers of this cabinet located in a bathroom. A "Flexalum" chrome-aluminum blind divides the two areas, providing light and air circulation along with privacy. Photo courtesy of Flexalum Decor Blinds

This bathroom vanity cabinet has two basins. The cabinet is painted, with drawers a darker color than doors. Doors have touch-type latches. Drawers are opened by pulling on the top edge of the front. This style drawer is not recommended for a bathroom where children may leave hand and fingerprints. Photo courtesy of Armstrong Cork Co.

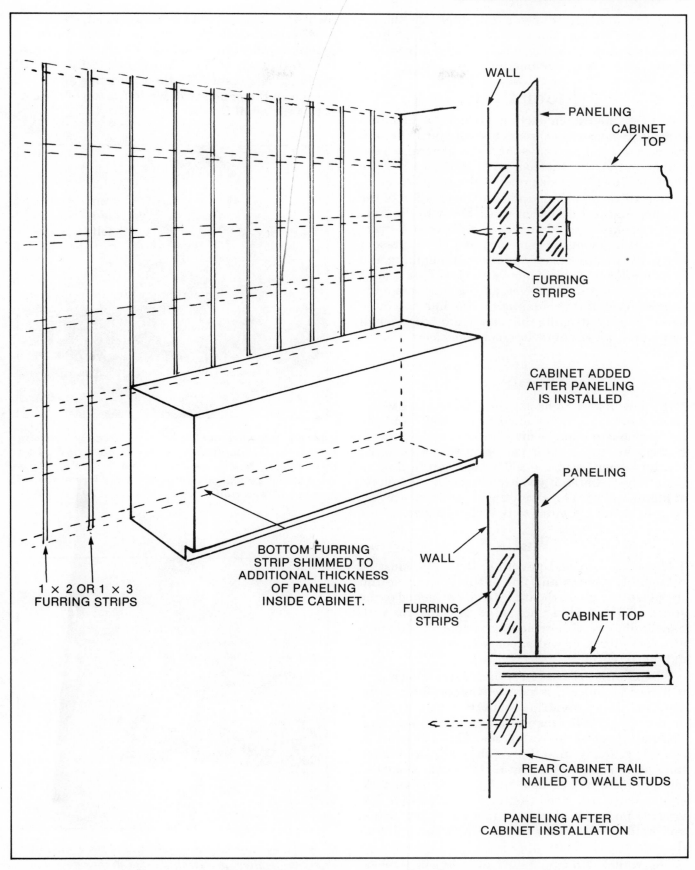

WALL

PANELING

CABINET TOP

FURRING STRIPS

CABINET ADDED
AFTER PANELING
IS INSTALLED

1 × 2 OR 1 × 3
FURRING STRIPS

BOTTOM FURRING
STRIP SHIMMED TO
ADDITIONAL THICKNESS
OF PANELING
INSIDE CABINET.

PANELING

WALL

FURRING STRIPS

CABINET TOP

REAR CABINET RAIL
NAILED TO WALL STUDS

PANELING AFTER
CABINET INSTALLATION

If walls are flat and smooth with plasterboard firmly attached, paneling can be applied with adhesive. All dirt, loose paint, or paper must first be removed when adhesive is used.

is highly unlikely that you will duplicate the arrangement shown. You can follow the guidelines and basic principles, however, as they apply to your particular room or circumstances.

Floor Plan

The first step in remodeling is to make a floor plan to scale. Because a bathroom is customarily a small room, use a larger scale than the generally used ¼-inch-to-the-foot. Instead, go to ½, ¾, or 1 inch-to-the-foot. The larger size makes planning easier.

Your drawing should indicate the location of the existing fixtures and their sizes. Draw in the cabinets you plan to build and/or install. Keep the vanity basin in about the same position as the present one to avoid unnecessary additional plumbing and long, inefficient runs of hot water pipe. This is not a hard-and-fast rule, however, as you can extend the existing piping with adapters to flexible polybutylene (PB) plastic piping that can be snaked through walls and under cabinets much like electrical wiring.

Fixtures

If the walls are to be paneled, the existing water closet tank (if it is fastened to the wall) and the lavatory basin must be disconnected and removed. If there are no shut-off valves in the lines to the lavatory basin and the toilet, now is the time to install them. Later, if you need to repair the faucets or plumbing, you can shut off just one fixture rather than shutting off water to the whole house.

Walls

If you plan to add paneling, the walls must be reasonably smooth and flat. If this is the case and the plaster or plasterboard is firmly attached to the studs, you can apply any kind of paneling with panel adhesive. Before using the adhesive, remove dirt, loose paint or wallpaper with a wire brush or dull putty knife.

Where walls are uneven or the plaster is loose, you will need furring strips to which the paneling can be attached. Space the strips about 16 inches on center, or as detailed in the instructions with the paneling, and nail them to the wall studs. The strips can be spaced vertically, directly over the studs, or horizontally across them. Horizontal strips can be spaced more than 16 inches, depending on the panel-maker's instructions. Keep the furring strips in a flat, vertical plane by placing shims under low spots, and holding the shims in place with nails driven through the furring strips.

The wall behind a cabinet need not be paneled because the existing wall can serve as the panel back. In this case, let the paneling run down about 2

inches below the top of the base cabinet, and behind any exposed ends of the cabinet. Where furring is required under the paneling, use the arrangement in Detail A, where the cabinet is installed after the paneling is finished. If the cabinet is already in place, run the paneling down to the top of the cabinet as in Detail B.

The vanity cabinet must be level, so check the floor with the aid of a straightedge piece of lumber, or a 24- or 36-inch level. Note low spots and mark them for placement of shingle shims. Photo courtesy of Western Wood Products Association

Mark the location of the cabinet on the floor, then tack shims to the floor, positioning them so they do not project beyond the cabinet. Photo courtesy of Western Wood Products Association

Framing for a vanity cabinet is much like that for kitchen cabinets. The main difference is the top, with a provision for basins.

CLEATS
NAILED TO WALL

1 × 8
STOCK

DRAWER CUT-OUTS

27 ¾ "

1 × 2S   1⅝"

4¼"

1 × 2S

NAILED TO PARTITIONS
AND 1 × 8

CLEATS FOR
DRAWER SLIDES

1⅝"

¾ " PLYWOOD

CLEATS

⅜ " × ⅜ "
RABBET

¾ " × 1½ "

PARTITIONS

⅜ " PLYWOOD

24" TO 32"

3⅝"

2 ¾ "

3¼ "

20 "

¾ " × 3⅝ "

3⅝"

20 "

NOTCHED AT PARTITIONS

MOLDING IF
NEED TO CLOSE GAP

4 "

2 ¾ "

CLEATS ON
TWO SIDES

Vanity Cabinet

It is absolutely necessary that the vanity cabinet be level, so shim up the floor at low spots so the bottom rails of the cabinet are firmly supported at points no more than 24 inches apart. The shims should not project beyond the cabinet base, so first mark on the floor the exact location of the cabinet, then use a level and straightedge to locate the necessary shims.

To build a vanity cabinet like the one shown in the example, follow the detailed drawing. The ends and partitions can be edge-glued solid stock or plywood. Partitions are identical, but the end panel is different. The horizontal piece at the lower front rail that provides a toe space is rabbeted at the back edge to accept the bottom of the cabinet. Notches are cut at the front for the upright members. Assemble the end panel and partitions with the bottom rear and front rails, along with the top rear rail, then set the cabinet in position. Nail the back rails to the wall studs or furring strips. If one end of the cabinet joins an adjacent wall, use cleats to support the cabinet top

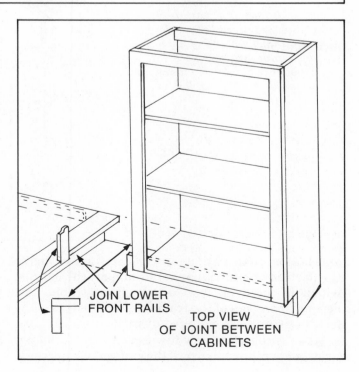

JOIN LOWER
FRONT RAILS

TOP VIEW
OF JOINT BETWEEN
CABINETS

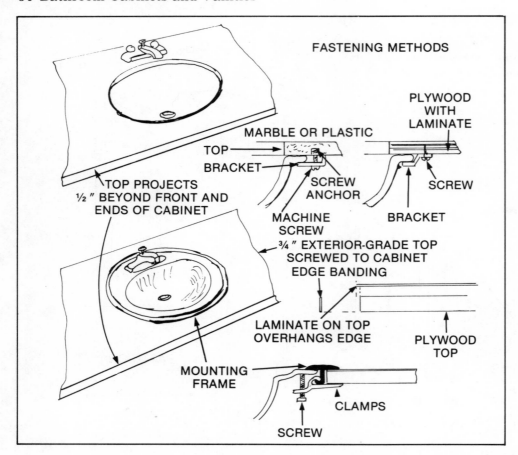

FASTENING METHODS

MARBLE OR PLASTIC

PLYWOOD WITH LAMINATE

TOP
BRACKET
SCREW ANCHOR
MACHINE SCREW
SCREW
BRACKET

TOP PROJECTS ½" BEYOND FRONT AND ENDS OF CABINET

¾" EXTERIOR-GRADE TOP SCREWED TO CABINET EDGE BANDING

LAMINATE ON TOP OVERHANGS EDGE

PLYWOOD TOP

MOUNTING FRAME

CLAMPS

SCREW

Vanity basins come in two main types. Those that fasten to the top of the counter and are held with a stainless-steel ring and clamps are called self-rimming basins. The other type that is attached to the underside of the vanity top and is held in position with screws and brackets, is called an under-the-counter basin.

This drawer is a variation of the "standard" construction shown in the chapter describing drawers used in kitchen cabinets. The back is fitted in vertical dadoes cut in the sides.

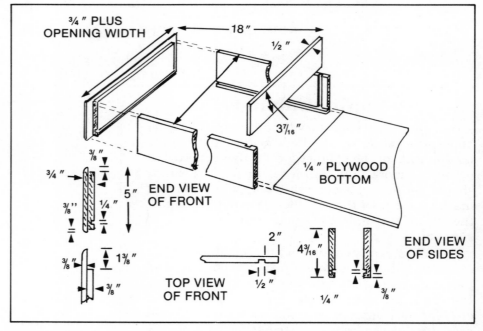

¾" PLUS OPENING WIDTH

18"

½"

3⁷⁄₁₆"

¼" PLYWOOD BOTTOM

¾"

⅜"

¼"

5"

END VIEW OF FRONT

⅜"

⅜"

1⅜"

⅜"

2"

½"

TOP VIEW OF FRONT

4³⁄₁₆"

¼"

⅜"

END VIEW OF SIDES

and bottom instead of a panel. Cleats are nailed to the partitions and end panel to support the bottom, which is cut next. Nail on the front frame. The vertical members of the frame cover the edges of the partitions and are centered over them.

Make cutouts in the wide, top front rail to form drawer openings, then nail the end vertical pieces to this rail. Use cleats to support the drawer slides. Cleats on partitions and at cabinet ends are of different thicknesses, so they will be flush with the ends of the drawer cutouts.

If you have restricted space in your bathroom, it may be necessary to reduce the width of the vanity cabinet a bit. In this case, however, be sure there is

A large mirror in the bathroom, especially where there are two basins in the vanity, is practical. The mirror also makes the room look bigger and lighter. Photo courtesy of Tile Council of America

enough room between the basin and the back rail for the faucet. There are several sizes of round and oval basins, which permit some flexibility in their position in the countertop.

Countertop

If your woodworking skills are limited, or your workshop space is not adequate, you can get a cabinetmaker to cut a countertop to size and cover it with plastic laminate in your choice of color and pattern. If you want to handle the project yourself, use ¾-inch plywood cut so it extends ½ inch beyond the front and exposed ends of the cabinet. Add a filler strip as detailed. Fasten the top to the cabinet with countersunk flathead screws or use angle brackets underneath. The brackets permit easy removal of the top should that ever be necessary.

Sand the plywood clean and remove sanding dust with a tack cloth. Cut the laminate a bit larger than the top, as described in an earlier chapter, where applying laminate to countertops is detailed.

Should you choose one of the new decorated vitreous china vanity basins that is attached to the underside of the cabinet top, it's a good idea to have a top of solid plastic or marble cut to the required size, with the basin opening cut in it. Marble tops are drilled for screw anchors with a special carbide-tipped bit.

China basins can also be used in a plywood top covered with plastic laminate. With the plywood top, the underside for a width of about 3 inches around the cutout is covered with fiberglass cloth and an epoxy resin. When this coating is dry, it can be sanded smooth for a good seal against the basin, and it will be waterproof.

Drop-in, self-rimming basins require a stainless-steel clamping ring held in position by special clamps. Caulking is applied under the edges that contact the basin and top. Excess caulking is wiped away after the ring is pulled down tightly by the clamps.

If you use angle brackets to attach the top, you can install the basin before attaching the top. This makes the job a lot easier, and the brackets also assure that in later years you can remove the top to change the basin or replace the laminate if you change the bathroom decor.

A narrow end cabinet can be built between the vanity cabinet and the water closet to utilize every bit of space. A cabinet like this can be installed as detailed, but allowance must be made for the narrow cabinet when building the vanity cabinet. Rather than a partition next to the drawer cutout and the door opening, just a drawer-support strip is installed, so all of the corner space can be utilized. Note that both the cabinet top and flooring extend

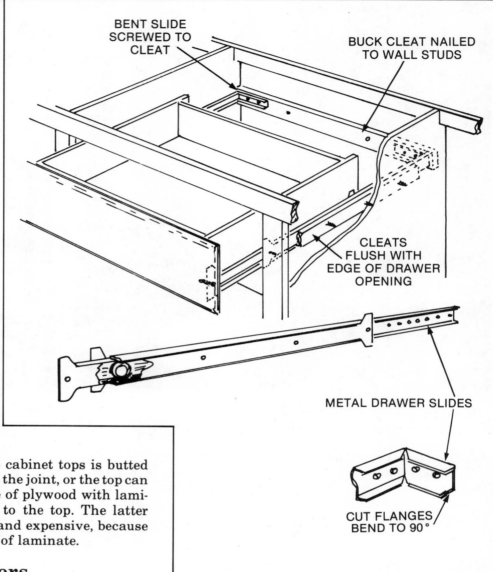

BENT SLIDE SCREWED TO CLEAT

BUCK CLEAT NAILED TO WALL STUDS

CLEATS FLUSH WITH EDGE OF DRAWER OPENING

METAL DRAWER SLIDES

CUT FLANGES BEND TO 90°

For any kind of drawer, ball-bearing slides make operation much easier. Various types are available, so always read instructions packed with them. Make all drawers a size that provides proper clearance for the devices.

to the adjacent wall.

The laminate on the two cabinet tops is butted tightly together to minimize the joint, or the top can be cut as an L-shaped piece of plywood with laminate trim already applied to the top. The latter method is time-consuming and expensive, because there is considerable waste of laminate.

Drawers

Drawings in the chapter on kitchen cabinets show a variation of the standard method of making drawers. In this variation, the back sets on the top of the bottom but is held in two dadoes cut vertically in the sides.

For easy drawer operation in any kind of cabinet, metal slides with ball-bearing rollers are best. And they do eliminate the need for wooden drawer guides, which simplifies drawer construction.

The metal slides are screwed to the lower edges of the sides of a drawer and to cleats on the cabinet partitions and ends. Slides of this type vary in construction and in details of attachment, but usually are made in lengths that are cut to fit a standard-sized cabinet. The type shown has flanges that are notched in a V-shape where the bend is made, and the bent ends are screwed to the back of the cabinet, or to a cleat on the wall if there is no back in the cabinet.

Doors

Doors for the bathroom cabinet can be any of the types described and detailed in the chapter on kitchen cabinet construction. Most mechanical door catches require the use of knobs or pulls, but you can eliminate the pulls by using "Tutch-Latches." With this latch you push a door to close it, push again to open it. This type latch is ideal for doors that are decorated with a wallcovering or cloth. It's a good idea, however, to screw on a square or rectangle of clear plastic where the door will be touched to open or close it. The plastic will protect the decorator material from being soiled by hands or fingers and can easily be wiped clean.

Period-design pulls, if you wish to use them, are available in antique brass or bronze finishes. You also can get carved-wood pulls if they will enhance your decorating scheme.

Bedroom Built-ins and Shelves

Built-ins and cabinets are ideal for a bedroom, because it generally is one of the smaller rooms in the house and has the largest piece of furniture—the bed. Other storage units like dressers, chests and closets require even more floor space.

The logical first step in planning a remodeling job in a bedroom is to figure a way to minimize the bulk of a bed. You probably do not want to actually reduce the size of a bed, but by building it in, and making it do service for something other than just a sleeping platform, you can increase the size of the available floor space and storage areas.

One basic example is to build a bed in a corner of the room, making it a bit higher than standard. The space underneath can then be used as cabinets with shelves and drawers. This may allow you to eliminate a dresser or chest of drawers that is taking up several square feet of floor space.

A built-in bed, depending on the style and design, is basically a platform on top of a box to support a mattress. It is possible to use both a box spring and a mattress, but the resulting bed would be quite high. In most cases just a mattress is used; modern units can be obtained in soft, medium, and firm, as well as extra-firm types; an innerspring mattress underneath has little or no effect on the resiliency of the mattress.

Keep in mind when you are designing and constructing a built-in bed that the bed must be made at frequent intervals. Many housewives find built-in and bunk beds a real problem when it comes to fitting sheets, blankets, and pillows on them. Because they are built-in, you cannot walk around them, so you have to work from just one side. This means wrestling with the far side of the mattress to tuck in sheets and blankets.

Do not consider placing any built-in bed against the wall if the mattress will be wider than a single bed, which measures 39 inches wide and 75 inches long. A youth-bed mattress or an all-purpose mattress is even better, as you can buy this type in lengths of 72 inches and widths of 27, 36, and 39 inches. These mattresses are sold by larger mail-order houses and some furniture stores.

If you are going to use a new mattress for a built-in, be sure to have it on hand before you start your building. The platform should be just a bit wider and longer than the mattress, especially if there are sides on the platform.

Be sure to allow space around the mattress for the thickness of a mattress cover, if one is used, plus the two sheets, blankets, and the spread. You want a nice, easy fit, not one that is cramped.

A built-in bed is basically a cabinet and can be made of ¾-inch plywood. If the room is paneled, you might want the bed to be of a contrasting hardwood-plywood, or to match the wall paneling. Veneered plywood ¾ inch thick is a bit expensive, so it makes more sense to build the bed of ¾- or ⅝-inch fir plywood, to which you brad and glue the same ⅛- or ¼-inch paneling used on the walls.

A couple of the built-in beds shown have been covered with wallpaper; when this is done you need a smoother surface than plywood. A smooth-surfaced particleboard can be used. This wood-base material comes in a variety of thicknesses. Alternately, use ½- or ⅝-inch plywood, to which ⅛- or ¼-inch hardboard is glued. The smooth side of the hardboard is faced outward to accept the wallpaper or other wallcovering material.

If a bedroom is located in a converted attic, floor space is more critical than on the lower floors. A built-in bed can be positioned under the low portion of the slanting ceiling, leaving the higher part of the ceiling for activities that require standing up. Storage can be built under the bed and at one or both ends.

If space is really a problem, you can make the bed like an oversize drawer that slides into the low part of the wall. The bed can move into the wall its full width, if space allows, or it can be designed to project partway to provide daytime seating. The recess into which the bed slides should be dust-tight and well ventilated, so the bed stays clean when it is stored.

For really simple construction, you can build a rough frame of 2 x 4s to which you glue and brad the wall paneling. A sheet of plywood should support the mattress. The plywood can be as thin as ½ inch if you have enough crosspieces to provide adequate support.

If you want to spend some time and money on the bed cabinet, you can build large drawers and install them with heavy-duty ball-bearing slides. Less complicated are large boxes mounted on casters that roll on the floor. Strips of wood on the floor can keep the casters aligned with the drawer opening and assure easy action. Build the drawers of ½-inch or heavier

This bed has an eight-drawer pedestal consisting of ¾-inch plywood and a standard, lightweight frame built of 2 x 4 stock. Photo courtesy of Wallcovering Bureau

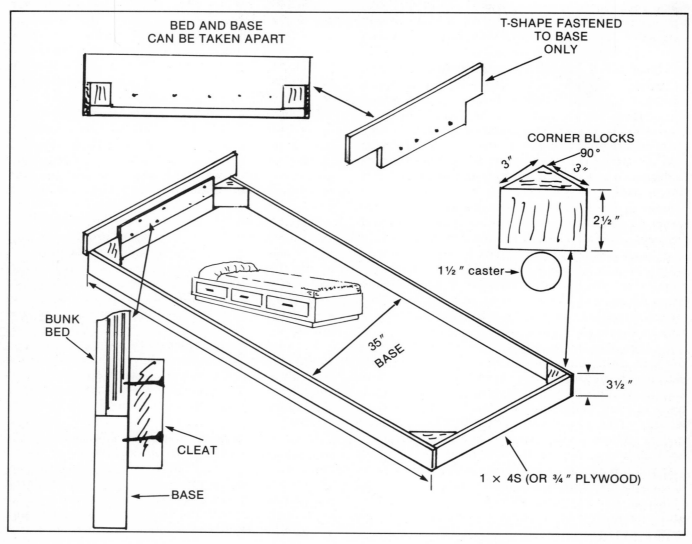

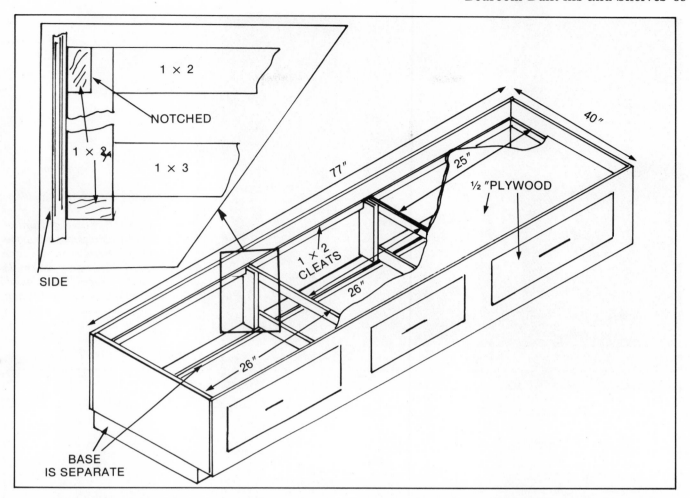

SIDE

1 × 2

NOTCHED

1 × 2

1 × 3

BASE
IS SEPARATE

77"

40"

25"

½ "PLYWOOD

1 × 2
CLEATS

26"

26"

This standard, lightweight framing for a bunk bed can be made to set in one place on a base, or the base can be fitted with spherical casters so the bed can be moved. Both long sides have toe space, so the bed can be turned either way or used in the center of a room. Ends are flush

plywood or particleboard to resemble large boxes. The faces of the drawers can be covered with wall paneling or wallpaper, depending on room decor and personal preference.

In a small bedroom you can utilize a walk-in closet as a sleep-in alcove. This would be suitable for a youngster. A child can store his or her clothes in a chest of drawers and a tall cabinet for coats and other items that must be stored on hangers.

Another way of utilizing every bit of space in a small bedroom is to use ready-made unfinished cabinets and furniture. Select items that provide the most storage and utility. In the room shown, a corner desk is flanked by a dressing table with a lift-up top on one side, while cabinets are stacked on the other side. The fairly compact units provide generous storage space and display shelving, along with a desk for homework, letter writing, or drawing.

An added touch is wall covering on the wall at the head of the bed, that matches the spread, and the valance on the ceiling positioned a couple of inches

with the base; bunk and base can be fastened together with a strip of wood at each end. Alternately, a T-shaped piece of wood is fastened to the base inside corner blocks to prevent the bunk from moving sideways or end-to-end.

from the walls.

If you have converted or plan to remodel your basement to add living space, consider adding a bedroom with a built-in bed. In the basement bedroom shown, the beds are simple platforms made by cutting ¾-inch plywood to the required size and trimming the edges of the plywood with 1 x 2s. "Legs" for the outboard ends of the beds are frames of 1 x 2s covered with paneling. The headboard end of one bed is directly against the wall, while the other bed is a bit longer so the mattress is about a foot away from the wall. The space at the head of the bed is a good display area.

Both beds can be used as seating during the day, and the shelf that joins the two beds can serve several purposes, including acting as a seat.

A clever touch is a pair of colonial-style doors to close off the basement window. You might want to consider one or two pairs of doors on other walls as doors to handy cabinets built into interior partitions.

To provide more floor space in a children's bedroom, bunks can be built into what was a walk-in closet. A simple frame of 2-inch lumber supports sheets of plywood on which mattresses are placed. Facing of bunks is ⅜-inch plywood flush with wallboard that also is ⅜ inch thick. The wallcovering is applied directly to bunk facings. Photo courtesy of Wallcovering Bureau

The structure of the bunk is framed much like wall assembly with 2 x 4 and 2 x 6 lumber. It would not be difficult to install drawers under both top and bottom bunks. Framing of 1 x 2s would be sufficient.

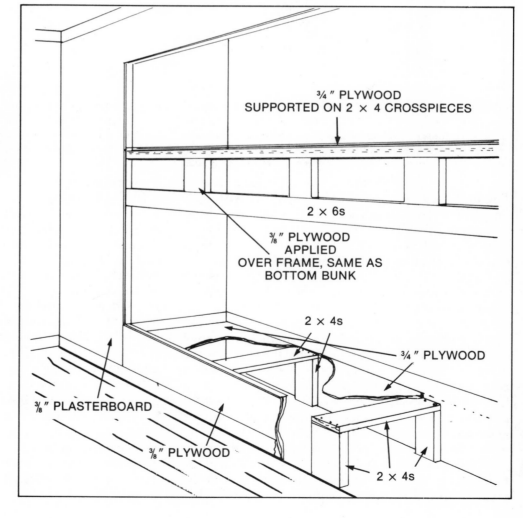

¾" PLYWOOD
SUPPORTED ON 2 × 4 CROSSPIECES

2 × 6s

⅜" PLYWOOD
APPLIED
OVER FRAME, SAME AS
BOTTOM BUNK

2 × 4s

¾" PLYWOOD

⅜" PLASTERBOARD

⅜" PLYWOOD

2 × 4s

The storage bunk in a child's room has several shelves for toys, and when the mattress is lifted, more hidden storage space is available. Photo courtesy of the National Gypsum Co.

A quick way to create "built-ins" is to buy units of unfinished furniture and fit them against the walls of the room. Here a corner desk is combined with a dressing table, that has a lift-up top, and storage cabinets with doors and open shelves. Photo courtesy of Mary Carter Paint Company

These built-in bunk beds have ample storage beneath the lower bed. A built-in desk below the window is fashioned in the same manner as the bunk bed. The bed and desk are covered with the same washable wallcovering. Photo courtesy of National Gypsum Co.

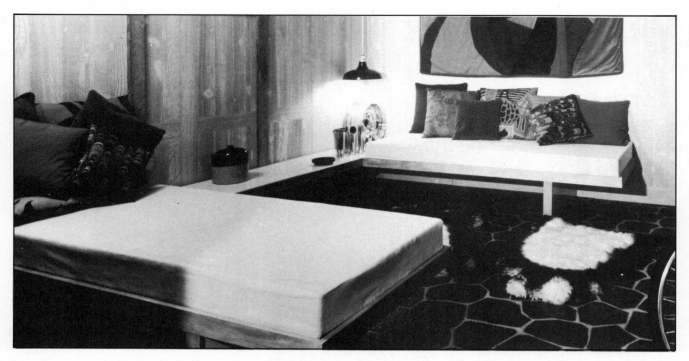

A new remodeled bedroom in the basement provides a sleep and lounging area. Built-in beds are all but indestructible. Mattresses are 5-inch foam units covered with zippered denim slipcovers for easy care. Walls are covered with easy-to-clean hardboard paneling. Photo courtesy of Masonite Corporation

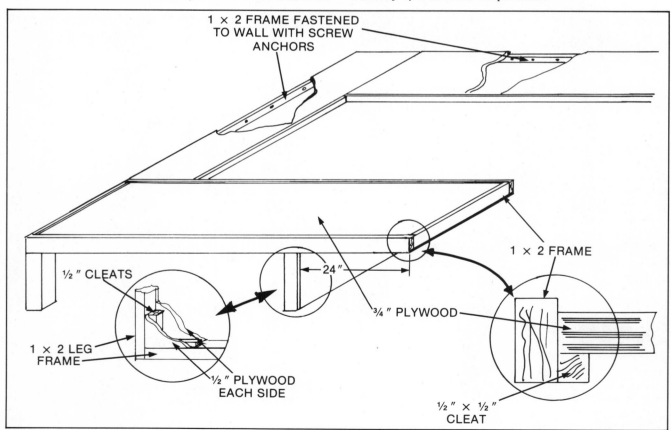

Bunk beds are simply sheets of plywood supported in 1 x 2 frames. One bed is longer than the other, so there is space at the head. The shorter bed is nearer to the doorway to provide a walkway into the room. Note that the "legs" for the beds are set back from the ends, in cantilevered fashion. This could provide additional storage space.

Shelving

If you don't want to get into projects as ambitious as the ones previously described, a simple shelving arrangement around a window can provide some storage. Buy stock 1 x 6, 1 x 8, 1 x 10 or 1 x 12 pine shelving. If you plan the shelving setup and make a rough drawing, it is quite possible the lumberyard or home center will have a man who can cut the pieces to length for you. You can put it together with hammer and nails and forego any sawing and problems with sawdust. You can be assured that the boards will have been cut square and true.

If your assembly stands firmly on the floor, and the floor is level, you will need only a couple of finishing nails or screws driven through the vertical portions of the shelving into the window trim. This makes it easy to remove for painting, papering, or moving.

Even simple shelving should have a toe space which can be made by nailing a length of 1 x 2 across the back and front of the setup to support the bottom shelf. Set the front 1 x 2 back about 1 inch. If there is a heat register on the wall, keep your shelving an inch or two away from it on all sides.

Shutters with movable louvers make the window seem to be a part of the shelving, giving a "cabinet" look when they are closed. The shutters are painted the same color as the shelves.

Pastel-toned paneling converts unfinished attic space to a place for the young sportsman to sleep and study, plus ample storage area. Lights over the built-in bunk are the inexpensive clamp-on type. They eliminate the need for installing permanent lights and can be moved to where they are needed. Photo courtesy of U.S. Plywood Div., Champion International

Attic construction varies, but general principles are the same; knee walls are furred to provide means of nailing up paneling and the "roof" over the bunk is framing covered with plywood. Trim at lower edge of paneling at the top of the bed is 1 x 4 or 1 x 6 to which 2 x 2 is glued and nailed. This provides an excellent place to clamp lights.

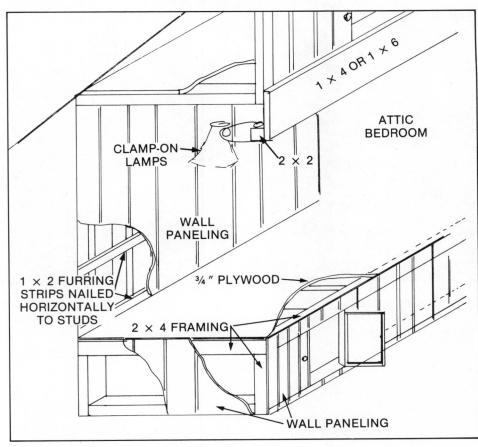

CLAMP-ON LAMPS

1 x 4 OR 1 x 6

ATTIC BEDROOM

2 x 2

WALL PANELING

1 x 2 FURRING STRIPS NAILED HORIZONTALLY TO STUDS

¾" PLYWOOD

2 x 4 FRAMING

WALL PANELING

Built-ins need not be elaborate. Here, shelving is assembled from stock pine shelving, glued and nailed with butt joints. The assembly is fitted around the window and heat register, and the shutters on the windows appear to be a shelving element. Photo courtesy of Wallcovering Information Bureau

How to Work with Plywood

Probably no building material is as versatile as plywood, and for the home craftsman, the large, flat panels provide an inexpensive, extremely strong wood product that can be used for hundreds of projects and purposes.

The cross-laminated veneer construction of plywood provides more stability than lumber, which is subject to twisting, cupping, and warping. Plywood may be used for paneling, partitions, doors, furniture, cabinets and built-ins, shelving, fences and wind screens, patio decking, outdoor storage units, and almost any project imaginable.

Characteristics

For the home craftsman there are two basic types of plywood: interior grade and exterior grade. The interior type has a water-resistant glue used between the laminations, while exterior-grade plywood has glue that is completely waterproof.

For cabinets and built-ins, the interior grade is adequate, with the exception that an exterior-grade plywood should be used on countertops that will be subjected to a lot of moisture like those in the bathroom. Plastic laminate or ceramic tile generally will prevent moisture from reaching the plywood on which it is applied. If you find that any counter on which you work shows signs of water damage, use exterior-grade plywood when you replace the top.

Birch plywood used for cabinets, or any hardwood-faced plywood, will come with one "good" side and one "bad" side. Both sides of hardwood-plywood are free of knots, splits and checks, and either side can be exposed.

Softwood plywood comes in grades, such as A-A, A-B and so on. For most construction, where one side will not be seen, A-D is sufficient. Where the inside of a cabinet will be seen occasionally, an A-C or A-B should be used. A-grade is smooth and paintable, with neatly made repairs permissible. B-Grade is solid-surface veneer with circular repair plugs and some knots permitted. When you get to C-Grade, there can be knotholes to 1 inch and occasional knotholes 1½ inches, providing the total width of all knots and knotholes within a specified section does not exceed certain limits. Limited splits are permitted. C-grade plgd (plugged) is an improved C-grade with splits limited to ⅛ inch in width and knotholes and borer holes limited to ¼ x ½ inch. The poorest grade is D-Grade, for which knots and knotholes up to 2½ inches in width, and even larger, are permitted within certain limits. Limited splits are permitted.

The grade marks on plywood will help you choose the kind you want, but a glance at both sides of a sheet will quickly tell you if it will be suitable for the job.

Working with Plywood

As with any kind of work, planning is important when you use plywood. If you will make a lot of cuts in a sheet, first make a rough work drawing so

When cutting plywood with a handsaw, have the good side up and support the panel so it doesn't sag. The saw should have 10 to 15 points per inch. If you want to minimize splintering on the back side, clamp a piece of scrap lumber to the plywood and cut it along with the plywood.

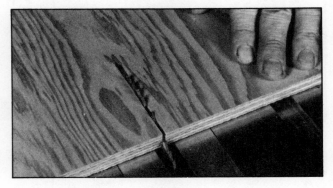

When cross-cutting or ripping on a table saw, or cross-cutting on a radial-arm saw, the good side of plywood should be up. When ripping on a radial-arm saw, the good side is down. The basic idea is to have the good side facing into the teeth of the blade as it rotates.

you can get an idea of how you can cut with the least waste. Most projects will require that the good face grain runs the long way of any piece you cut. And don't forget to allow for the saw kerf, which usually is about ⅛ inch. If you overlook that ⅛ inch and cut four pieces, you are ½ inch off.

When sawing plywood, the idea is to have the good face positioned so the teeth of the blade cut into it. With a handsaw this means the good face up, and the same is true when cutting on a table saw. With a radial-arm saw the good face is up when you cross-cut, as the blade is pulled back through the stock in a "climbing" cut. When you rip on a radial-arm saw, the good face is down, as the blade then cuts on the "upstroke."

A portable electric saw also cuts upward, so the good face of the plywood should be positioned down. An electric jig saw (saber saw) cuts on the upstroke also, so the good face should be down, and all marking done on the back side of the plywood.

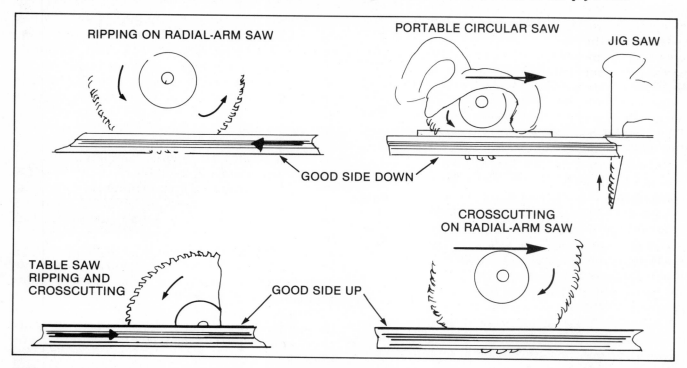

With an electric jig saw, put good side down; the same is true when using a portable circular saw.

You can reduce the weight of a project but still keep it strong by using a frame of solid lumber over which thin plywood is nailed and glued.

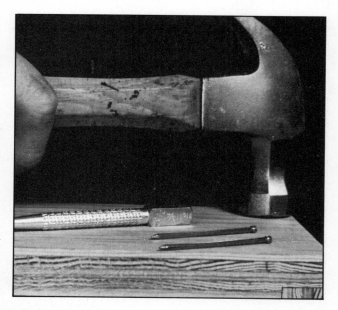

Rabbet joints are neat and strong, and provide additional gluing surfaces. Any permanent joint in plywood should be glued. Ordinary white glue is adequate for most jobs.

If you must plane the edges of plywood, make sure the plane blade is very sharp, and take shallow cuts. Plane from each end of an edge toward the middle to avoid splintering at the ends. The use of a planer or plywood blade will produce a cut that is so smooth it won't even need sanding. If at all possible, it is best to avoid planing.

Joints

Even the very best glue cannot make up for a sloppy joint, so "dry-fit" pieces of a project together to make sure they meet properly. When using ¾-inch plywood, or thicker, you can glue and then nail or screw plain butt joints. If the plywood is thinner, then use a glue block inside each corner. Framing made from solid stock permits using lighter plywood, which enables you to keep down the weight. Thinner plywood also is less expensive, as long as you don't spend too much on the framing stock.

Rabbet joints provide a bit of extra gluing surface and are quite neat, as only a thin edge of the plywood shows. The miter joint (not shown) is the neatest, but does require precision cutting at the correct angle and proper fastening.

If you have a table or radial-arm saw, dadoes make neat joints for slide-in shelves in cabinets. Use a dado blade to make the cut in one pass, both for width and depth. With some care and a fence clamped to the plywood, you can use a portable circular saw with a dado blade to cut the grooves.

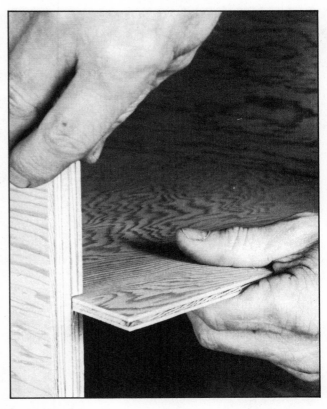

Dado joints made with a power saw enable the production of neat shelves. The dado blade, either the multiblade type or one of the newer, adjustable types, makes the dadoes in one pass. If you make the dadoes a sliding fit, it should not be necessary to hammer the shelves into the slots.

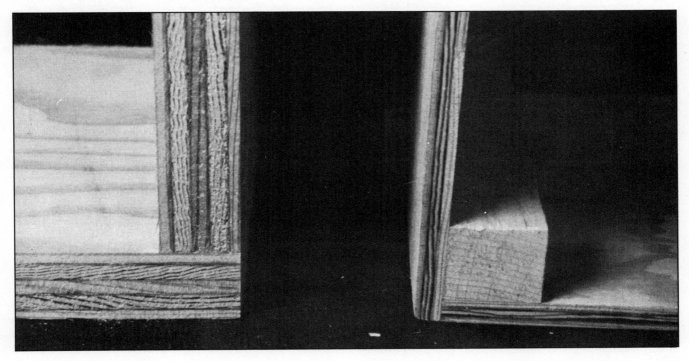

Butt joints are simplest to make, as at left, and often are used with ¾-inch plywood. When thinner material is used, you should include a glue block inside the corner.

Flathead woodscrews are used when you want a joint that is stronger than one made with nails. A No. 8 screw is used on ⅝- and ¾-inch plywood, No. 6 with ⅜- and ½-inch plywood, and No. 4 with ¼-inch plywood. Use the longest screw practical. This depends on the thickness of the backing material.

Nail size is determined by the thickness of the plywood. For ¾-inch plywood, use 6-penny casing nails or 8-penny finishing nails. With ⅝-inch plywood, drive 6- or 8-penny finishing or casing nails. When ½-inch plywood is being nailed, use 4-penny or 6-penny nails. When nailing ⅜-inch material, nail sizes are 3- or 4-penny. You can drive ¾- or 1-inch brads or 3-penny finishing nails to attach ¼-inch plywood. Where the material will not show, you may use 1-inch blue lath nails.

Glue and Fasteners

All plywood joints should include glue as well as fasteners, unless the project is one that will occasionally, or frequently, be disassembled. Nail size is determined by the thickness of the plywood. Finishing nails are usually used, but casing nails that are like oversize finishing nails are used for extra strength. When nailing close to an edge, predrill the nail holes with a bit that is slightly smaller than the nail diameter. Drill just through the first piece of plywood and start into the second. Nails are spaced 6 inches apart for most projects, but closer spacing is required for thinner plywood to prevent slight buckling between nails. Once again, be sure to use glue as well as nails.

For a really strong joint, use flathead wood screws. Both screws and nails should be countersunk and

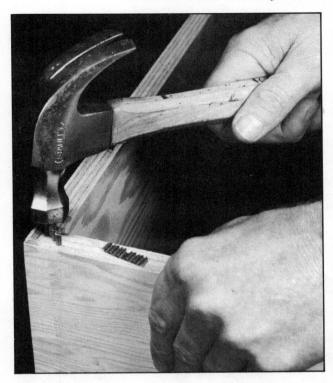

Ordinary corrugated fasteners can be driven into a corner to hold a miter while the glue sets and also to provide reinforcement for the joint. Use one at each end, if possible.

All nails and screws should be countersunk and heads covered with wood putty. Fill the holes so the putty is above the surface, then sand it flush when it dries. If screws drive hard, wipe them on a bar of soap or a piece of paraffin.

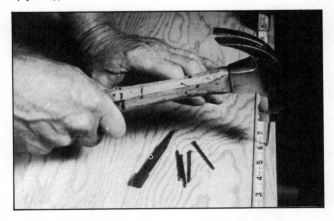

For most projects, space the nails about 6 inches apart. When you are using thinner plywood, as over framing, space the nails closer to avoid any buckling, and always use glue.

On some projects where nails will be near the edges, predrilling is a good idea. Use a drill bit slightly smaller than the nail diameter, or use a nail with the head cut off as the "bit." A hand or electric drill can be used.

the heads covered with wood putty. Or, use plugs cut from scraps of plywood. Pieces of dowel will make a contrast to the plywood and create a pegged, colonial look.

A quick and easy way to hold miter joints is to use plain corrugated fasteners at each end. Sheet metal screws are better for some joints than wood screws (as with particleboard) although you cannot get them as long as wood screws, and greater length may be required for some joints. Where really great strength is required, use nuts and bolts. This also is true of items that need to be disassembled frequently.

For most jobs, ordinary white glue is fine. "Carpenter's" glue is a bit stronger and has a quicker "tack." For outdoor assemblies made with exterior-grade plywood, definitely use a two-part waterproof glue that is mixed just before it is used. Both white glue and carpenter's glue are water-resistant, but not waterproof. They will fail when exposed to constant weathering, rain, and snow.

Edge grain of plywood soaks up glue quickly, so apply one coat and let it get tacky, then apply a

Dry-assemble a project to check for proper fit of all joints, then disassemble and apply glue.

Apply glue with a brush or stick, or directly from the container in the case of white glue. End grain absorbs glue quickly, so apply a light coat, let it dry for a few minutes, and then apply a second coat just before assembling the joints.

While nails and screws will draw a glued joint together, clamps make an even tighter connection. Use shims of cardboard or wood under the clamp pads to prevent marring the wood surface.

second coat just before you joint the pieces. Screws or nails will hold a joint once they are driven, but during assembly regular clamps will assure that you get the project square and the joints tight. Nails or screws hold the joints tightly after the glue has set and the clamps have been removed.

When you hang cabinets on a stud wall, use a thin plywood back in the cabinet. Screws can then be driven through the back into the wall studs through the plaster or plasterboard. For hollow masonry walls, use toggle bolts or "Molly" anchors. The "Molly" devices permit removing and replacing the screw, while the toggle portion of a toggle bolt drops inside the wall when the screw is removed.

For poured concrete and other solid masonry, you can use "glue-on" holders that have nails or screws that project for attachment. Also, there now are cartridge-actuated nail and stud drivers that can be rented to attach furring strips to masonry. The cabinet or other item is then attached to the furring strips with wood screws.

Standard stud walls allow hanging cabinets by driving screws through the cabinet backs into the studs. Locate one stud by tapping on the wall, then measure 16 inches to find the next. The 16-inch spacing is not always consistent near a corner or next to a door or window.

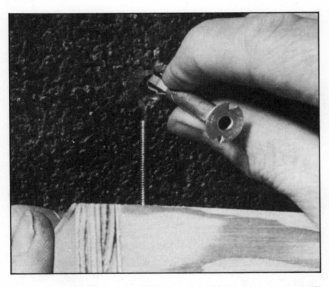

If you are hanging cabinets on hollow masonry walls, you will need to use toggle bolts or "Molly" fasteners as shown. The advantage of the "Molly" fastener is that you can remove and replace the screw once the fastener is in place.

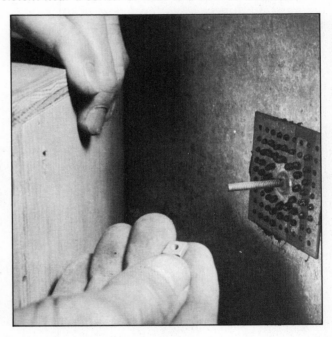

On poured concrete and other solid masonry, "glue-on" masonry anchors are required. Some types are simply projecting nails onto which the wood is driven, then the nail clinched over. The fastener shown is a threaded screw. A nut is turned on it to hold the cabinet to the wall.

Hinges

Door hardware for plywood should be a type that permits driving the screws into face grain; screws driven into edge grain do not have much strength. "H-hinges" and "H-L" hinges are strong and provide a colonial or Early-American look to a project. For larger doors where three hinges are required, use a pair of "H-L" hinges with an "H-hinge" at the center.

Semi-concealed hinges do a nice job on lipped cabinet doors. Screws are driven into the face grain for good strength. Semi-concealed loose-pin hinges (which permit easy removal of the door by pulling the pins) show only the pin barrel when the door is closed, and thus look like regular butt hinges. Screws, however, again are driven into face grain for good holding strength. Hinges with concealed pins mount on the sides of a cabinet, so that no facing frame is necessary. They are ideal for a cabinet of modern design. Only the pivot is visible when the door is closed.

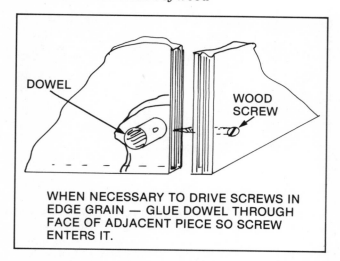

DOWEL

WOOD SCREW

WHEN NECESSARY TO DRIVE SCREWS IN EDGE GRAIN — GLUE DOWEL THROUGH FACE OF ADJACENT PIECE SO SCREW ENTERS IT.

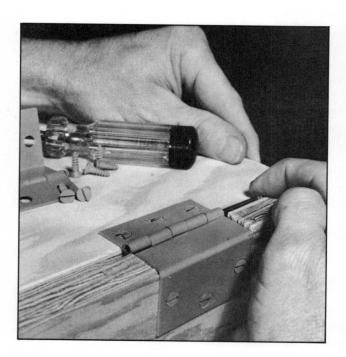

Loose-pin hinges that are semi-concealed look much like ordinary butt hinges when the door is closed, because only the barrel shows. Again, the screws are driven into the face grain of the plywood to provide excellent holding power.

Surface-mounted hinges are attached easily, require no mortising, and add a decorative touch. One pair of H or H-L hinges is sufficient for most cabinet doors. For larger doors, use a pair of H-L hinges with an H-hinge in the middle.

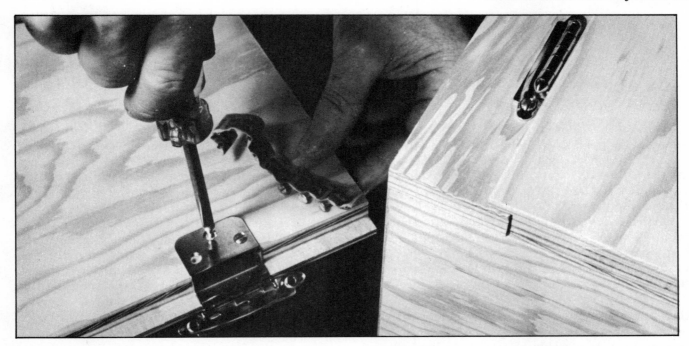

Lipped, overlapping doors hang neatly with semi-concealed hinges. These offset hinges are ideal for plywood, as the screws are driven into face grain. The edge grain of plywood does not provide the holding strength of face grain.

When mounted directly onto the cabinet side, concealed-pin hinges provide a neat, modern appearance to flush doors. Because no facing frame is required with this type of hinge, cabinet construction is simplified. Only the pivot is visible from the front with the door closed. A pair of these hinges is used for a small door, and three for a larger door. Three hinges are called a "pair and a half."

How to Work with Particleboard

Because the average home craftsman doesn't know much about it, particleboard is not often used for home projects such as cabinets, although the manufacturers of furniture and other products have considered it their favorite material for quality items for many years.

Particleboard is a man-made material created by mixing particles of wood with a resin binder, then compressing the mixture and heating it to produce a uniformly dense panel. The light tan panels are flat, have no grain, and are completely free of knots.

Edges of particleboard are tight, with no voids that sometime occur in softwood plywood. Particleboard is heavy for a wood product. It's about 40 percent heavier per volume than pine lumber, and 25 percent more than softwood plywood. Both sides of particleboard are smooth.

There are some disadvantages to particleboard, as no material can be all things to every craftsman. Comparing particleboard to some other cabinet-making materials in ¾-inch panels of 4 x 8 feet, we find that particleboard has a higher surface hardness than A—B softwood plywood, A—2 birch plywood, and 1-inch (¾ inch net) pine lumber of clear and better grade. When it comes to workability, soft pine lumber is easier than particleboard to saw, plane, rout, and drill. Because of the glue lines, both kinds of plywood are more difficult than particleboard to work. Although particleboard can be worked with regular tools, the resin in it makes it tougher on cutting edges.

Stability of particleboard is very good. It originally was developed for manufacturers of tabletops, cabinet doors, and cabinet tops who demanded an inexpensive, stable wood core for their products.

Vertical compression strength is also good. To compare horizontal strength with that of other materials, consider this comparison: pine shelving will support a load on 36-inch centers; plywood is safe on 30-inch centers; particleboard is heavier and has shorter wood fibers and so requires spacing of no more than 24 inches for the same load. On 24-inch centers, a ¾-inch particleboard will support 70 pounds per square foot and deflect just ¼ inch. This kind of strength is more than adequate for a set of heavy encyclopedias.

When it comes to comparison of edge finishing, lumber is clearly superior. Edges are smooth, tight and require no filling, although end grain may in some cases. Particleboard is second. You can some-

times obtain it with filled round or square edges, or with applied wood edges. Plywood would be the last choice, for it has voids that need to be filled, and there is edge grain that must be concealed by filling with veneer tape or solid wood.

Another advantage is that particleboard can normally be stained or painted with no additional preparation. For a top-notch job, wipe the surface with thinned paste filler and sand it. Plywood and lumber have problems of raised grain, and you have to work to hide color differences in solid lumber. Patches and repairs on softwood plywood are difficult to conceal without painting.

When it comes to money, the cost of particleboard can make you a confirmed user in a hurry. According to Louisiana-Pacific, a major producer of lumber, plywood, and particleboard, the price of plywood with two good sides is more than double the same size piece of particleboard. When you compare it with the same amount of pine lumber, you are talking three times the cost. Birch plywood is about four times the price of particleboard.

Particleboard is made of thicknesses from ⅛ to 2 inches. Panels can be as wide as 5 feet and as long as 26 feet. Density of the product can range from 28 to 62 pounds per cubic foot. During the manufacturing and blending of the panel materials, wood preservatives, termite-resistant chemicals, and even fire-resistant substances may be added.

Furniture manufacturers use particleboard in both high- and low-priced items for core stock to be painted or varnished. It also is used under plastic laminate, sheet vinyl, and wood veneer. Because it is uniformly dense, it makes an ideal material for hi-fi speaker cabinets.

Most specialty boards are not sold in your local lumberyard. You will probably find medium-density boards from 42 to 45 pounds per cubic foot in 4 x 8-foot panels of standard thicknesses. These thicknesses are ⅜, ½, ⅝, and ¾ inch, with ⅝ inch being the most widely available.

Working with Particleboard

When you work with particleboard two things quickly become obvious, especially if working with power tools. First, instead of sawdust that presents little problem, you create a gritty shower of particles. Safety glasses or a face shield are a must. Second, because of the high concentration of abra-

With a sharp blade on a table or radial-arm saw, a "self-edge" is relatively easy to develop. Note that the bottom self-edge would be ideal to increase front thickness of a countertop.

Molding can be used to edge particleboard. From top to bottom: outside-corner trim; plain screen trim; half-round molding; ¾-inch cove molding for ¾-inch particleboard. Use of moldings eliminates the need for filling and finishing rough particleboard edges. All photos in this chapter courtesy of Louisiana Pacific

sive resins in the particleboard, tools dull quickly. For larger projects, such as cabinets, it's worthwhile to get carbide-tipped saw blades, router bits, and shaper cutters. These special tools work faster, make smoother cuts, and stay sharp much longer. You'll find the carbide tools will stay sharp many times longer when working with regular wood, making them a good investment.

Power bits, twist drills, hole saws, and fly cutters, along with most standard woodworking tools, work beautifully with particleboard. Be sure to back up particleboard when drilling to prevent splintering

Carbide tools are almost a must when working with particleboard. Unless you are doing a small job, an investment in carbide-tipped saw blades and router bits is well worth the cost.

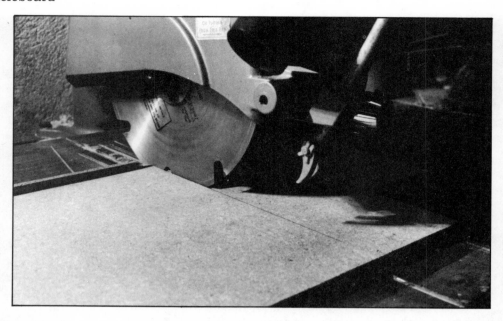

You can purchase some particleboard shelving with an edge-filled bullnose (bottom); you can glue or veneer tape (second from bottom); you can add solid moldings as shown previously; or you can fill with wood putty and sand smooth.

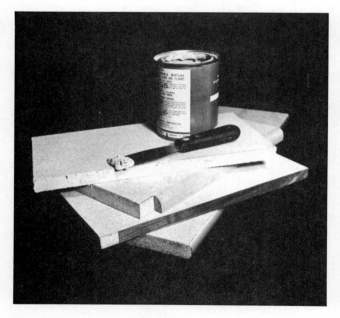

Some typical rabbeted corner joints. It must be stressed that with particleboard there must be a mechanical fastening combined with glue. This means that the more glue surface you can provide, the better off you are.

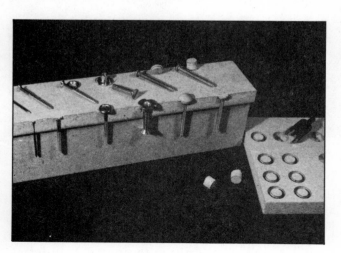

Fastening hardware and finishing techniques, left to right: finishing nail, wood screw both countersunk and puttied over; wood screw with finishing cup washer; T-nut and machine screw; sheet metal screw with button to cover counter-bored sheet metal screw; sheet metal screw with head in counter-bored hole that is then plugged with length of dowel or cut plug. At right is a plug cutter that can be used in a drill press or portable drill to create plugs from the stock being used.

on the back side. This is true of plywood or solid lumber as well.

While routing is easy on particleboard, you'll notice that the core is not as dense as the area near the surface; it may require filling before a finish is applied.

When you fill the edge of particleboard, make the filler a creamy consistency for the edges, but thin it to paint-like consistency for the faces. You can eliminate the need for filler on the edges by using solid stock, molding, or veneer tape.

Fastening and Gluing

Be sure to provide maximum gluing surfaces when making joints in particleboard, as shown for half-lap, mitered, and splined joints. Strengthen corner joints with inside glue blocks where possible. Nails are used only to hold the joints until the glue sets, as particleboard has very little nailholding strength. Countersink finishing nails and cover the heads with wood putty. Wood screws are better than nails, as they are for any wood product, but sheet metal screws work best in particleboard. These

Illustrated are mitered-corner systems that reduce or eliminate the need for filling or finishing the rougher core material of particleboard. From top to bottom: interior glue block with a miter corner; splined miter corner; rabbeted-miter corner, all of which provide generous glue surfaces.

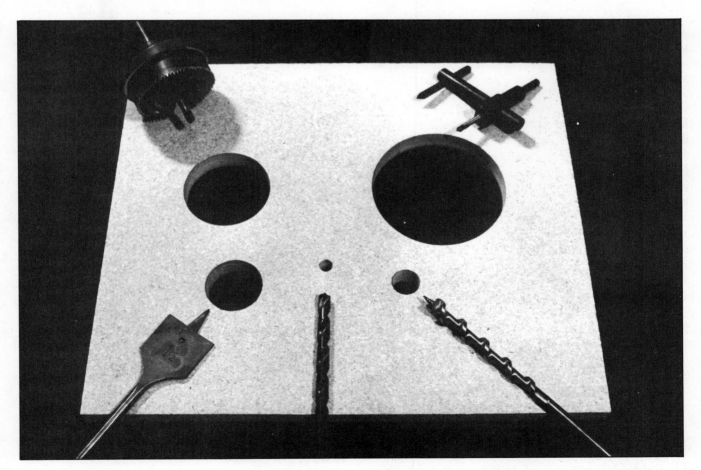

Particleboard can be sawed, drilled, and shaped with regular woodworking equipment, either hand or powered. Particularly when drilling, however, it's important to supply a firm backing to prevent material from tearing-out on the back side.

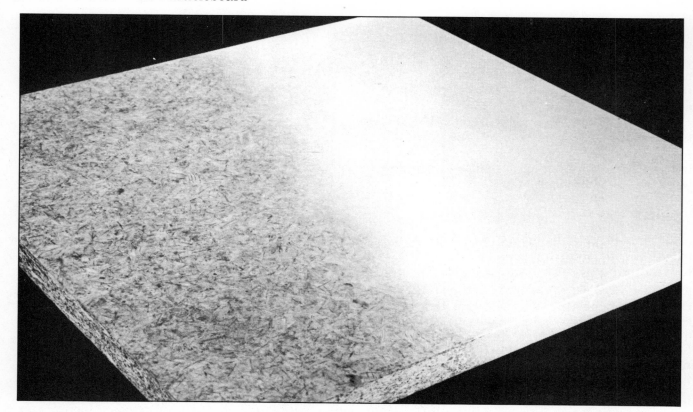

screws have wider, deeper threads that "bite" into the particleboard. Either kind of screw for particleboard should be longer and thinner than you would use in solid lumber. Turn the screws in firmly, but don't overdo it or you'll strip the threads. A drop of white glue in each screw hole helps. The glue seals the particleboard and enables the threads to make a more solid cut in the material.

Nail heads and screw heads are countersunk and covered with wood putty that is sanded smooth when dry. As an alternative to putty, counterbore the holes and then fill the recesses with short plugs or pieces of dowel, or wooden "buttons" that create a colonial look. Where joints are to be occasionally taken apart, use plated finishing washers under the screw heads.

When you join two pieces of particleboard so only one side will be exposed, such as rails and stiles in doors or cabinet frames, corrugated fasteners or "Skotch" fasteners can be used, along with glue. All permanent particleboard joints should be glued.

Any hardware that can be used with plywood or solid lumber can be used with particleboard. Pulls and handles used for doors and drawers, however, should be the "bolt-through" type rather than being screwed to the surface. If possible, use sheet metal rather than wood screws. Surface-mount hinges; don't screw them to the edges of particleboard. It takes only 160 pounds of pull to remove a sheet metal screw from the edges of particleboard, but 225 pounds to wrench it from the face.

Paint can be applied to particleboard with a brush, roller, or spray gun. Oil-base paints or lacquers are preferred over latex-base paints that tend to raise the grain and create a rough surface. While particleboard has no true grain, it is a wood product, and the various particles do swell when wet.

Hinges, pulls, and other standard hardware used on wood and plywood can be applied to particleboard projects; however, where wood screws are normally used, as for attaching hinges, sheet metal screws are recommended.

Applying Plastic Laminate

High-pressure plastic laminate is used on most countertops. It is available in a wide variety of solid colors, patterns, and even woodgrains. The laminate is made by assembling layers of paper and chemicals, then subjecting this "sandwich" to tremendous heat and pressure. The result is a dense, long-wearing material that is easily cleaned.

Like any material, however, after a number of years, it begins to show signs of wear; it becomes scratched and dull, and there may even be bulges and bubbles. You can replace the doors on your cabinets with new ones, and paint or stain the facings, but an old base countertop will never look good until you replace the plastic laminate.

Much has been said about renewing laminate and the problem of removing the old contact adhesive from the plywood or particleboard contact once you have stripped off the old laminate. Removing the laminate is fairly simple: you just find a loose edge, slip a putty knife under it, and start pulling.

The problem is with the adhesive. Unfortunately, up to now, there has not been an efficient way to remove old adhesive. If you apply new adhesive over the old, you never really get a good bond, and the new laminate will start to come loose and buckle within days.

The only practical renovation is to completely replace the countertop. There are two ways countertops are attached: (1) with wood screws countersunk down through the top, and the screw heads exposed when the old laminate is pried off, or (2) with screws driven up through the framing into the underside of the top. This latter is actually the better method, whether the top is plywood or particleboard.

Either method works. The choice is up to you. The main advantage of the screws being driven from underneath is that you can get at them to tighten or loosen them, which might be necessary if you want to shim up one corner or end of the countertop to level it. If the laminate has already been applied, the screw heads are covered, and there is nothing you can do.

To get back to renewing a countertop: if it is a sink counter, shut off the water, disconnect the water lines and drain. Pry off the laminate, if necessary, to get at the screws holding the top to the framing. You can use the old top as a pattern, if you plan to use the same exact dimensions. If you plan to change the dimensions, you will have to measure and score the countertop.

Using plastic laminate with hickory wood-grain pattern is a beautiful way to add easy-care durability to your kitchen, while complementing the natural beauty of hardwood cabinets. Photo courtesy of Wilsonart

Cut the top to size from plywood or particleboard, then glue and nail on 1 x 2-inch strips around the edge (or variations of this as detailed in the chapter on kitchen cabinets). Tools you will need for renewing the countertop are those found in most home workshops. You can save on a lot of cutting by having the lumberyard cut the top material to the sizes you have already determined. This makes transportation easier. If you have a portable router, you can purchase a special plastic-laminate cutting setup. If not, you can use a hand-powered trimmer with carbide cutters in it. Files also can be used; if you trim the laminate to about ⅛ inch oversize, then file it down. We'd recommend the manual trimmer. It is not too expensive, will last a lifetime, and will save time and trouble.

Most countertops are about 24 inches wide. To renew a countertop, you purchase laminate 30 inches wide and a foot or two longer than you think necessary, to allow for waste and trimming. Cut the lami-

A close-up of a sink that was renewed by replacing the countertop with plastic laminate. The backsplash is also covered with wood-grain plastic laminate.

Tools required for replacing a countertop include electric jig saw, portable router (or hand laminate trimmer), electric drill, hand saw, file, screwdriver, and hammer.

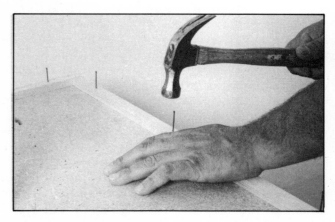

After ¾-inch particleboard or plywood is cut to the size of the countertop, strips of 1 x 2 stock are nailed to the edge to create a thickness of 1½ inches.

nate on a table or radial-arm saw, using a slightly dull plywood-cutting blade. Wear safety goggles or a face shield. Particles of laminate are hazardous to your eyes.

Cut a strip of laminate about ⅛ inch wider than the edge of the countertop you have created, including the strips along the edges. Check the fit and apply contact adhesive to the laminate and countertop edge. Follow the instructions on the adhesive container. There also will be listed a maximum time, after which the adhesive will not hold. Should you manage not to apply the laminate within this limit, simply apply another coat on both the countertop and the laminate, then apply the laminate.

Press the laminate firmly against the edge of the top, then go along with a block of wood and hammer and tap firmly to make sure the laminate adheres. Even better, use a flat roller that will squeeze out air bubbles and assure full contact.

Use a router with laminate trimmer, or a hand trimmer, and cut the top edge of the laminate flush with the countertop. Next, cut the laminate pieces for the countertop, allowing at least ⅛ inch extra in width and length. Check the fit, then apply the adhesive to both surfaces.

Because of the large surface, you need help in aligning the laminate before pressing it onto the adhesive. Use dowels or metal welding rods between the countertop and laminate until you have the laminate properly aligned, then remove the supports one at a time as you press the laminate to the countertop. This method is easier and better than using newspaper or wrapping paper, as is some-

Plastic laminate is cut about ¼ inch oversize for the top of the counter, and then positioned to make sure it is the proper size. It then is removed and contact adhesive is applied to the back of the laminate and the top of the counter. On plywood or particleboard, it's a good idea to apply two coats of adhesive, as wood products are somewhat porous.

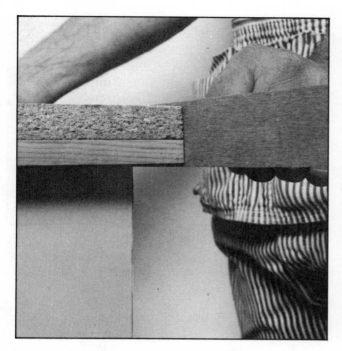

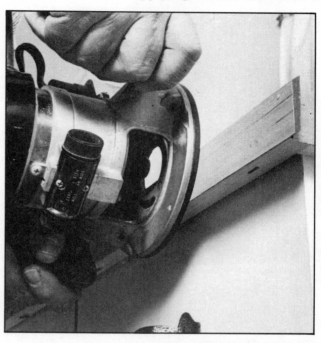

A laminate strip for the edge is cut and applied first. It is allowed to project slightly above the top surface of the new countertop. It is applied with contact adhesive.

If you have a portable router with a laminate cutter, it can be used to trim the upper edge of the laminate flush with the top of the counter. A fine file also can be used, if held flat on the countertop.

After adhesive is applied, plastic laminate is placed on the countertop, but kept above it by small-diameter dow-

els or pieces of welding rod to prevent the adhesive from "grabbing" until you have the piece positioned correctly.

A router with a special laminate cutter can be used to trim laminate on the top flush with edge strips. It also can be filed or trimmed with a hand-powered laminate trimmer.

The backsplash is covered separately, then holes are drilled through so wood screws can pass through it and be driven into the back edge of the countertop. Apply latex caulking on the back edge of the countertop, so there will be a waterproof seal between it and the backsplash.

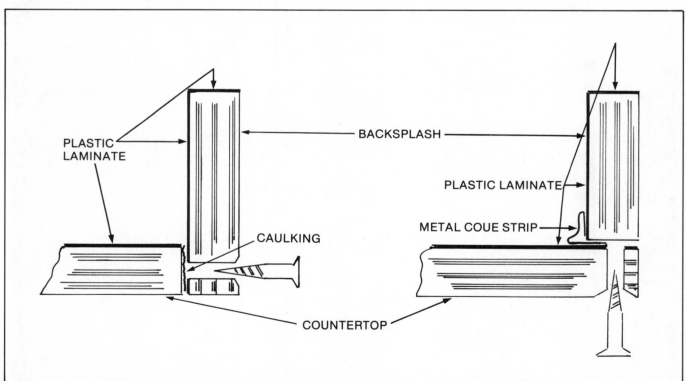

PLASTIC LAMINATE

BACKSPLASH

PLASTIC LAMINATE

METAL COUE STRIP

CAULKING

COUNTERTOP

The backsplash is covered with laminate separately, then is attached with screws before the counter is attached to the frame by driving screws from underneath.

Caulking or a metal strip is used between the counter and the backsplash. The backsplash can be attached to the countertop in either of these two ways.

times suggested, because the paper can stick to the glue in spots.

Trim the edge of the laminate on the top as you did on the edge, using the same tools and methods.

If you have a backsplash on the countertop that will also be covered with laminate, cover it separately, then attach it to the back edge or top (as described in the chapter on kitchen counters). Clearance holes for the screws are drilled through the plywood or particleboard and the laminate, so the backsplash can be attached. A bead of caulking should be applied along the edge of the backsplash to seal it against water.

A cutout is required for the sink, and you can use the old countertop for a pattern, or perhaps you will want to locate the sink differently. Mark the outline, drill a hole in each corner, then cut out the opening with a portable electric jig saw.

Replace the sink by reversing the steps for taking it out. Turn on the water to check and repair any leaks. Do the same with the drain.

Since your plastic laminate required replacing, you may want to replace the sink also. This is not a difficult job and, since you already have the old sink removed, half the job is already done. As with many household appliances, sinks are now designed for do-it-yourself installation.

Complete instructions are packaged with such sinks, so be sure to study them carefully. The cutout for the new sink will be described, and in some cases a paper template will be provided.

Use the original countertop to determine the size of the hole for the sink. If a new sink is to be installed, get the proper size from the instructions that come with it. Drill your starting hole inside the outline you draw.

The sink cutout is made with a portable electric jig saw. Make sure the sole of the saw is clean and has no burrs that might mar the surface of the new laminate.

Check the sink in the opening to make sure it fits properly. File off any projections or rough spots. Apply caulk- *ing around the edge of the cutout, then reinstall sink. Or install a new one following the instructions.*

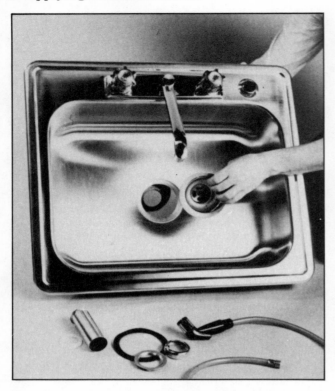

Do-it-yourself stainless-steel sink installation starts with mounting the faucet, spray, and drain fittings before the sink is fitted in the opening in the countertop. Photo series courtesy of Neptune Lifetime Sinks

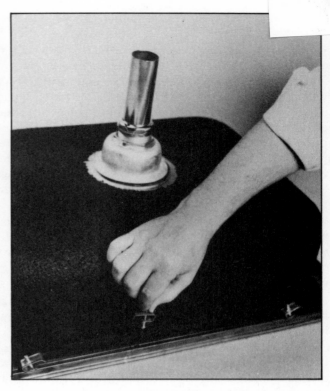

Step two is to fit into the sink rim the "one-hand" mounting clips. A continuous bead of caulking then is applied to the underside of the rim.

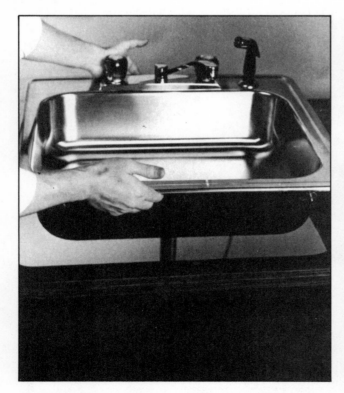

Lower the sink into the countertop cutout. It is wise to have someone help with this part of the installation.

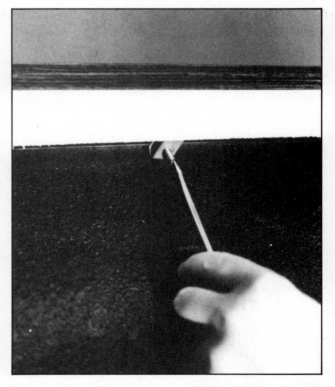

With the sink in the cutout, position the clips, then tighten them with a screwdriver. Make sure the caulking squeezes out under the complete rim on the countertop. Wipe off the excess and make the plumbing and drain connections.

Index

Metric Conversion Tables

Length Conversions

fractional inch	millimeters	fractional inch	millimeters
1/32	.7938	17/32	13.49
1/16	1.588	9/16	14.29
3/32	2.381	19/32	15.08
1/8	3.175	5/8	15.88
5/32	3.969	21/32	16.67
3/16	4.763	11/16	17.46
7/32	5.556	23/32	18.26
1/4	6.350	3/4	19.05
9/32	7.144	25/32	19.84
5/16	7.938	13/16	20.64
11/32	8.731	27/32	21.43
3/8	9.525	7/8	22.23
13/32	10.32	29/32	23.02
7/16	11.11	15/16	23.81
15/32	11.91	31/32	24.61
1/2	12.70	1	25.40

feet	meters	feet	meters
1	.3048	8	2.438
1½	.4572	8½	2.591
2	.6096	9	2.743
2½	.7620	9½	2.896
3	.9144	10	3.048
3½	1.067	10½	3.200
4	1.219	11	3.353
4½	1.372	11½	3.505
5	1.524	12	3.658
5½	1.676	15	4.572
6	1.829	20	6.096
6½	1.981	25	7.620
7	2.133	50	15.24
7½	2.286	100	30.48

inches	centimeters	inches	centimeters
1	2.54	5	12.70
1¼	3.175	5¼	13.34
1½	3.81	5½	13.97
1¾	4.445	5¾	14.61
2	5.08	6	15.24
2¼	5.715	6½	16.51
2½	6.35	7	17.78
2¾	6.985	7½	19.05
3	7.62	8	20.32
3¼	8.255	8½	21.59
3½	8.89	9	22.86
3¾	9.525	9½	24.13
4	10.16	10	25.40
4¼	10.80	10½	26.67
4½	11.43	11	27.94
4¾	12.07	11½	29.21

Common Conversion Factors

	Given the number of	To obtain the number of	Multiply by
Length	inches	centimeters (cm)	2.54
	feet	decimeters (dm)	3.05
	yards	meters (m)	0.91
	miles	kilometers (km)	1.61
	millimeters (mm)	inches	0.039
	centimeters	inches	0.39
	meters	yards	1.09
	kilometers	miles	0.62
Area	square inches	square centimeters (cm²)	6.45
	square feet	square meters (m²)	0.093
	square yards	square meters	0.84
	square miles	square kilometers (km²)	2.59
	acres	hectares (ha)	0.40
	square centimeters	square inches	0.16
	square meters	square yards	1.20
	square kilometers	square miles	0.39
	hectares	acres	2.47
Mass or weight	grains	milligrams (mg)	64.8
	ounces	grams (g)	28.3
	pounds	kilograms (kg)	0.45
	short tons	megagrams (metric tons)	0.91
	milligrams	grains	0.015
	grams	ounces	0.035
	kilograms	pounds	2.21
	megagrams	short tons	1.10
Capacity or volume	fluid ounces	milliliter (ml)	29.8
	pints (fluid)	liters (l)	0.47
	quarts (fluid)	liters	0.95
	gallons (fluid)	liters	3.80
	cubic inches	cubic centimeters (cm³)	16.4
	cubic feet	cubic meters (m³)	0.028
	cubic feet	liters	28.3
	bushels (dry)	liters	35.2
	milliliters	ounces	0.034
	liters	pints	2.11
	liters	quarts	1.06
	liters	gallons	0.26
	liters	cubic feet	0.035
	cubic centimeters	cubic inches	0.061
	cubic meters	cubic feet	35.3
	cubic meters	bushels	28.4
Temperature	degrees Fahrenheit	degrees Celsius	0.556 (after subtracting 32)
	degrees Celsius	degrees Fahrenheit	1.80 (then add 32)